ALONG THE
SAWDUST
TRAIL

Ivy Ruth Venden

Nostalgic Stories From the Golden Era
of Adventist Evangelism

Pacific Press® Publishing Association
Nampa, Idaho
Oshawa, Ontario, Canada

Edited by Jerry D. Thomas
Designed by Michelle C. Petz
Cover photos provided by Morris Venden

Venden, Ivy Ruth, b. 1898.
　　Along the sawdust trail : nostalgic stories from the golden era of Adventist
evangelism / Ivy Ruth Venden.

　　　　p.　cm.
　　ISBN 0-81631725-0 (pbk.)
　　1. Venden, Ivy Ruth, b. 1898.　2. Seventh-day Adventists—United
States Biography.　I. Title.
BX6193.V46A3　1999
286.7′092—dc21
[B]　　　　　　　　　　　　　　　　　　　　　　　　99-33763
　　　　　　　　　　　　　　　　　　　　　　　　　　CIP

99 00 01 02 03 • 5 4 3 2 1

<u>DEDICATION</u>

To my husband,
with whom I have traveled
for more than sixty years.
Without his work, this book
would not have been written.

CONTENTS

FOREWORD

My heart overflows with love for Jesus as I help prepare this manuscript for publication. How I love Him for giving me a praying mother, so gentle, so good, so kind. She died at age 91, having outlived all her peers. Among her things, we found this record of her life on the evangelistic ("sawdust") trail. It was written out by hand, perhaps only for her own reflection. Naturally, it has the flavor of the earlier years (1930s, '40s, '50s), but the gospel is still the old, old story that never grows old.

Morris L. Venden

How the changing years have found me
far away from thoughts of home.
Now no Mother bends above me
when the time for sleep has come.

But it brings my poor heart comfort
and it gives me peace within,

Along the Sawdust Trail

just to dream that I am little
and my Mother tucks me in.

As I kneel there with my brother
by the bed above the stairs,
And I hear our gentle Mother
whisper, "Boys, remember prayers."

Then she comes and kneels beside us,
"Father, keep them from all sin."
Oh, her kiss is tender, gentle
when my Mother tucks me in.

When at last the evening finds me
and the day of life is done.
All the things of earth that bind me
shall be broken, one by one.

Then, Oh Lord, be thou my comfort.
Calm my soul, Thy peace to win.
Let me fall asleep as gently
as when Mother tucked me in.

H.M.S. Richards

Foreword

"The wind bloweth where it listeth,
and thou hearest the sound thereof, but canst not
tell whence it cometh, and whither it goeth:
so is every one that is born of the Spirit"
(John 3:8).

This great truth, that was given to Nicodemus
by Jesus Himself so long ago,
you will understand more fully as you travel
with us along the Evangelistic Trail.

ABOUT THE AUTHOR

I was born Ivy Ruth Blackenburg in Minnesota on March 25, 1898. My mother was of English descent, and my father, John Blackenburg, was Irish and German. His parents were staunch Catholics, so my father was taught to give reverence to the priest and faithfully carry out the instructions of the church. His mother died when he was eighteen.

After her death, the priest frequently asked for money to pay for his efforts to get her out of purgatory. John was perplexed. He remembered her as a kind, loving mother, and it seemed to him unacceptable that she could suffer in the fires of hell. He came to the conclusion that the purgatory story was a money racket, so he left the Catholic Church.

Later, John Blackenburg met and married Abbie Wheeler, who was a Seventh-day Adventist. Even though he did not join the church until many years later, he respected my mother's religion and was always kind to his family. He worked very hard as a farmer, as well as in other lines of work.

I was their fourth child. Seven years after my birth,

my sister Zelda was born. She was my pride and joy, and I rocked her to sleep many times in my little red rocking chair. As we grew older, we were all taught to work. Any money that we made helped to pay for our clothes and schoolbooks.

In the fall of 1917, I went to Loma Linda and began to study for my career as a nurse. Each student was supposed to make a deposit of twenty-five dollars as an entrance fee. I did not have the necessary money, so I kept my distance from the business office. One day, Mr. Bowen, the manager, asked me to come into his office. He said, "Would you like to make your deposit today?"

I could only answer, "I am sorry, but I have no money."

He said, "Miss Blackenburg, didn't you know you would be expected to pay?"

With downcast eyes I replied, "Yes, but I thought if I got here you wouldn't turn me away."

He smiled as he said, "No, we would never do that." He arranged for me to do some extra work, and soon I had the twenty-five-dollar fee paid.

I graduated with the class of 1920. Not long after, I was called home to Idaho because of the illness of my father. About five years before, he had become a Seventh-day Adventist.

It was my privilege to care for him the last few weeks of his life. The hours I spent with him were very precious. The last night I was with him, I read Revelation 22:17: "And the Spirit and the bride say, Come. And let him that heareth say, Come. And let him that is athirst come. And whosoever will, let him take the water of life freely."

When I finished he said, "Oh, that is wonderful." He

squeezed my hand and fell asleep. I expect to see him again in the kingdom, where there will be no more dying and no more crying.

Not too long after, I married one of the finest men who ever walked this earth. He was an evangelist, and for many years, with his brother Dan and sister-in-law, Nellie, we carried on a delightful life with many blessings.

Now I want you to become acquainted with my husband, Melvin Venden, and his brother, Dan, as children, as college students, and as singing evangelists.

INTRODUCTION

Two boys, later known as the Venden Brothers, lived in a log cabin surrounded by many evergreen trees and beautiful maples in Trout Lake, Washington. Their home was about twelve miles from majestic Mt. Adams, whose summit was the weather gauge for the valley. When a cloud covered its peak, foul weather was expected.

The Venden boys, Dan and Melvin, along with their brothers and sisters, roamed the woods, stomping through snows in winter and gathering wildflowers in springtime. In those carefree days, they little sensed the concerns of their parents, Nels and Christine Venden, who carried the responsibility of feeding seven hungry children. Mother cared for the children, and Father worked away from home in construction.

Later the family moved to Washougal, Washington, where Nels built a good house and a large barn and did diversified farming. His boys helped him plant fruit trees and do the other chores around the farm. Their family was the first in that part of the country to have a bathtub with water piped into the house.

Along the Sawdust Trail

Inga Dorthea, who was next to the oldest in the family, worked away from home when she could. She became ill and for many weeks suffered severe pain. Doctors were scarce in those days, and the nearest one was many miles from where they lived. Finally, after much agony, she was laid to rest. In spite of their great sorrow, the family was relieved to know that her suffering was over.

(A few years ago, we stood beside her grave. We thanked God for the blessed hope of the resurrection when we will meet Inga Dorthea again).

Not long after Inga's death, Father Venden died. He had always been a strong man, but too much hard work had worn him down and at the age of forty-four, he was buried beside his precious daughter Inga. What a day that will be when there will be no more death, no more sorrow, and no more crying.

Now the older boys had to take their father's place. But before long, Mother Venden sold the home and the family moved away. Today, someone else is living in the house that her husband built. Someone else is eating the fruit from the trees her husband planted. Someone else is putting hay into the big barn.

Thank God a day is coming when "they shall not build, and another inhabit; they shall not plant, and another eat: for as the days of a tree are the days of my people, and mine elect shall long enjoy the work of their hands" (Isaiah 65:22).

When Dan and Melvin finished the academy, they were impressed to go to Walla Walla College and study for the ministry. They had no money, so they had to work their way. Obtaining an education was not easy under their circumstances, but finally they graduated and began their internship in God's work.

These two brothers had a vision of someday working together as an evangelistic team. This vision became a reality when they began their journey on the Evangelistic Trail, traveling from west to east and east to west.

CHAPTER ONE

The Trail Begins in Hood River

◆ ◆ ◆

Hood River is a city in Oregon built near the shore of the Columbia River. When my husband, Melvin, and his brother, Dan, teamed up to hold evangelistic meetings, this town was the first one on their list. The conference provided them with a portable tabernacle designed to be moved from city to city.

There was an Adventist church in Hood River but because of division among the members, attendance at the meetings was not good at first. Satan always has someone who tries to disrupt God's plans.

Another problem was a local woman by the name of Mrs. Whitman. She hated Seventh-day Adventists and would come to the meetings to see who was attending and then go to their homes criticizing the evangelists. She advised them to stay away from the tabernacle and also gave them literature written against Adventists.

One night my brother-in-law preached on the subject "The Man Who Came to the Wedding Without a Wedding Robe." This robe represents the righteousness of Christ and the importance of God's Law—including the keeping of the fourth commandment, God's holy Sabbath day.

Mrs. Whitman saw herself in that picture. Even though she had been talking against the meetings and our beliefs, through God's grace we became friends. After the meeting that night, my brother-in-law had the opportunity to talk with her. During their long talk, her heart was broken. She confessed what she had been doing and asked how she could make things right. He told her there was only one thing to do, and that was to go to each one of those people and confess how she had been mistaken. She should tell them that the evangelists had proven to her from the Bible that the Seventh-day Adventist beliefs were right. He assured her that we would all be praying for her. Her sincerity was genuine, and she did as he advised. Through the power of the Holy Spirit, a tragedy was turned into victory.

The attendance at the meetings increased. Mrs. Whitman was baptized and through her influence, a number of others became members of the Hood River Seventh-day Adventist Church.

The tabernacle was next moved to Trout Lake, Washington, a community on the Washington side of the Columbia River—about twenty-five miles from Hood River. This was the same Trout Lake where my husband was born and where he lived the carefree life of a child. He was thrilled to come back to his hometown as an evangelist! A suitable

The Trail Begins in Hood River

place was found for the tabernacle, and the meetings began.

When my husband was fourteen years old, he worked for a farmer named Mr. Arni. Melvin was an earnest Christian at that time, and he told Mr. Arni that he could not work on the Sabbath. He said he would help with the morning chores, but after those were completed, he would like to be free to go to his church.

One Saturday morning, Mr. Arni asked Melvin to harness the horses so that he could get out to the fields a little quicker. Melvin thought for a moment then said, "I can't do that because that would be helping you, Mr. Arni, to work on the Sabbath, which is God's holy day." Mr. Arni, a kind man, let Melvin go on to church.

But he had not forgotten the testimony of that fourteen-year-old boy, and night after night, the entire Arni family came to the evangelistic meetings. Along with others, they were baptized and became members of the Trout Lake Seventh-day Adventist Church.

While the tabernacle was being moved to The Dalles, Oregon, the Venden brothers held some meetings in White Salmon, a town halfway between Trout Lake and The Dalles. There they rented an old Baptist Church that had been empty for some time.

Melvin's oldest brother, Joe, who lived in the area, came to help get the church in shape for the evangelistic meetings. There were no Adventists in White Salmon, but the Lord saw some honest-hearted people who would accept the messages given by the Venden brothers.

Mrs. Bremer, the wife of the high-school principal, came with a friend of hers. She told us later on that while

Along the Sawdust Trail

sitting on one of those hard benches, she kept saying to herself, "I wonder if these men really believe what they are talking about." Finally through the work of the Holy Spirit, she freely accepted truth and was baptized along with her friend and her friend's daughter.

Mr. and Mrs. Wang and their daughter had been old friends of the Venden family. They came to hear these two boys who had grown to manhood with a burden on their hearts to save souls for God's kingdom. They were impressed with the evangelists' earnestness and zeal and made their decision in response to the call to become members of God's family.

Earl McCoy, his wife, and a number of others also decided for Christ, and a church of forty members was organized. For many years, they used the old Baptist Church as their meeting place. Now a beautiful church with an attractive stone front—which Melvin's brother constructed—stands in White Salmon as a testimony to the love and power of God.

The evangelistic team moved on to The Dalles. The tabernacle was erected, and the Venden brothers made ready to begin another crusade.

CHAPTER TWO

Transformed by God's Grace

◆ ◆ ◆

In 1930, the president of the United States declared all banks closed for a period of time. That year began the time known as the Depression. People with money in banks lost it. Those who owed money on their homes lost those as well. Men were out of work, and business was at a standstill. There was hunger in homes across the country, and many people stood in bread lines for the only food they would have to eat.

The Rosses

Mr. and Mrs. Ross had been doing well. They owned their own home and were in business, with forty thousand dollars in their savings account. They were not church folks. They were both members of a lodge. In fact,

Along the Sawdust Trail

Mr. Ross belonged to the highest order and had held various offices. Mrs. Ross was an active member also, leading out in many social functions.

God and the teachings of the Bible had no part in their lives. Mr. Ross often took the Lord's name in vain. He smoked and drank some and had a general feeling of security in the friendships of his associates. Yes, the Rosses were swinging high.

Then the Depression struck. Some lost thousands of dollars, while others gained financially. In many cases, the rich became richer and the poor poorer. In a moment, the accumulation of a lifetime could be swept away.

It happened suddenly to the Rosses. Their forty thousand dollars vanished! Mr. Ross and his wife were stunned. They were in confusion. How could they carry on their business without money? It became necessary for them to sell their fine home and move into more modest quarters.

The next year was a hard one, and business was very bad. Their supposedly good friends who still prospered forgot all about Mr. Ross and his wife, Nel. The lodge dues hadn't been paid, so, of course, they were not in good and regular standing there. Nel couldn't dress as well as she had, so the socialites shunned her. They were about to lose their home again, so they moved, this time into a most humble type of dwelling.

Discouragement settled down upon them. Mr. Ross drank more and smoked constantly. Nel became sick, and Mr. Ross developed a stiffness in his back, which made it hard for him to do common labor. He often gazed at the mighty Columbia River that flowed near their humble home, longing for relief from his troubles.

Transformed by God's Grace

Most often, Mr. Ross sat on a bench in a park in The Dalles, Oregon, whiling away the hours by exchanging vile stories with other dejected men. His frequent oaths could be heard by the people passing by. He became one of the most deplorable characters in the town. Some looked upon him with disgust and some with pity. It made no difference to him. His money was gone, his friends were gone, and now his health was slipping away.

About this time, an odd building was erected on a vacant lot. It seemed to be a church or tabernacle. Mr. Ross often passed along that street, and his curiosity was aroused. One day he noticed a sign out in front which read, "*Back to the Bible Campaign. Come and Hear the Venden Brothers.*"

"I suppose this is some crazy religion that has come to town," muttered Mr. Ross. "I sure don't want any of it."

One night he heard the singing. It didn't sound so bad. He thought perhaps he would just take a look inside. A young man stood up front leading the music. The people were singing with all their hearts. Mr. Ross slipped onto a bench in the back as the sermon began. This was new and strange language to him. He couldn't sit for long. He needed a cigarette, so out he went.

But there is power in the gospel! He kept hearing those songs and the words of scriptures from God's Holy Book over and over in his mind. A few nights later, he ventured into that tabernacle again. This time the other young man was leading the music. They seemed so happy! Could it be the religion that made them that way?

My husband (the young preacher) stood up to speak. Mr. Ross needed a cigarette, but he really hated to leave.

Along the Sawdust Trail

Still, he just had to have a smoke, so he puffed fast and hard, threw the stub on the ground, and self-consciously made his way back in. This time, he heard more of those wonderful words of life. But that vicious smoking habit suddenly seized him again. He reached for a "Lucky" and quickly made his way out to walk home in a kind of daze.

Nel was asleep, and he didn't want to awaken her. A peculiar feeling was creeping into his heart. For a long time he couldn't sleep. He felt almost frantic, and the air turned blue with smoke as he clipped the cigarettes off one by one. Finally, with an oath, he buried his face in his pillow, unable to understand these strange emotions.

A week passed before our friend Mr. Ross went to the meeting place again. This time, he sat a little nearer to the front. He knew the preacher saw him. In fact, he was sure the preacher looked straight at him. He wanted a cigarette desperately but decided to try and hang on a little longer. The speaker was reading from the Bible, "But God commendeth his love toward us, in that, while we were yet sinners, Christ died for us. For when we were yet without strength, in due time Christ died for the ungodly" (Romans 5:8, 6).

"Christ died for the ungodly," Ross said over and over to himself. "Could it be that He died for me?" He wished he hadn't sat so close to the front. He needed a cigarette badly, but he wanted to hear the rest of the story. He determined to stick it out. Suddenly, he began to tremble and shake. The minister was offering the closing prayer. Mr. Ross stumbled to the door and out into the darkness. His trembling hand fumbled for a cigarette. The next thing he was aware of was entering the door of his shack.

Transformed by God's Grace

Nel was sitting by the little heater. Her face was pale and haggard, and she almost shouted at her companion, "Where on earth have you been? You look scared and white as a sheet."

"Nel, I have been going to that tabernacle on L Street," Mr. Ross replied, "I really heard something tonight. The preacher read from the Bible that Christ died for the ungodly. Nel, do you think he meant me? The next time I go, I want you to go with me, Nel. They sing a lot and seem so happy there."

Sunday night found the Rosses at the tabernacle. Mr. Ross boldly took his wife well over halfway to the front. There they heard the special music by the two preacher brothers. The song's words rang over and over in Nel's ears, "They will never pay rent for a mansion, the taxes will never come due." Nel looked around, and everyone seemed so happy.

The sermon began, and she listened intently. It seemed to her that she had heard something like that somewhere, before. Mr. Ross nudged her, "Say, I've got to go for a smoke; stay here, I'll be back." Sure enough, back he came, and they stayed for the entire meeting.

That night, the preacher hurried to the back door to give the folks a friendly handshake. Mr. Ross and his wife followed the crowd toward the door, and to Mr. Ross, they moved much too slowly. The nagging desire for another cigarette kept him anxious, but the preacher was so friendly that for a moment Mr. Ross forgot his lifelong habit.

On the way home, they both were silent. As they entered the door, Nel whispered, "They will never pay rent for a mansion, the taxes will never come due." Mr. Ross

Along the Sawdust Trail

gulped hard as he said, "Let's go again tomorrow night."

Night after night found them at the tabernacle where great truths of the Bible were clearly portrayed. They learned of the love of God and the plan of salvation. They heard the sure and certain promises to the overcomer. They discovered the reward of the righteous. They sang songs of praise and found their burdens lifted and their hearts made glad.

Finally, by using all his willpower, Mr. Ross was able to sit through an entire meeting without a cigarette, though he had to have one as soon as he got out. Still, in his heart a peculiar love was developing for an individual he had never seen—the great God, the Creator of heaven and earth.

Mr. Ross realized that for years he had been taking this Man's name in vain, and he didn't want to do that anymore. One day as he sat on the park bench, an old crony let out an oath. To hear the Friend he had learned to love spoken of in such a way hurt Mr. Ross so much that for a moment he felt like fighting.

One night the preacher read from the Bible, "Though your sins be as scarlet, they shall be as white as snow; though they be red like crimson, they shall be as wool" (Isaiah 1:18). A call was made, and many came to the altar for special prayer.

Mr. Ross sat very still; then suddenly he took Nel by the hand and hurried toward the door. One of the preachers was there waiting to greet them, and this time the friendly handshake was a little different. The speaker looked into the tall, thin, old man's eyes with a look of compassion and repeated softly, "If we confess our sins, he is faithful and just to forgive us our sins, and to cleanse us from all unrighteousness" (1 John 1:9).

The next day the preacher visited at the Ross home. For a few minutes, they talked about the weather and the price of hay. By this time the preacher knew more about the lives of these two people than they dreamed he did. He had them on his prayer list, and he knew all about the terrific battle against smoking, as well as the struggle to refrain from using vile language.

He put his hand on Mr. Ross's shoulder and said, "Mr. Ross, we have been praying for you and your wife."

"You have!" Mr. Ross was startled, and tears began to gather. "I figured someone was praying 'cause something's been happening to this heart of mine. I don't understand it; when I hear men cussing and swearing now, it makes me sad. Thanks a lot for your prayers."

The evangelists continued to pray for Mr. Ross and his wife and for many others who attended their meetings and were having a hard battle against the enemy of souls. Certainly the dragon was wroth and was going forth to make war. Victories were being won, and many honest-hearted folks were taking their stand for the great Bible truths.

Meetings were held each Sabbath afternoon. The foundation stones had been laid. The wonderful love of Jesus and His sacrifice on Calvary was melting the heart of the hardest sinner. Finally one day, when a call was made for decisions, Mr. Ross hesitated a moment and then he and his wife walked to the front bench, tears of repentance coursing down their cheeks. For the preachers, it was a day of great thanksgiving. And they were certain there was joy among the angels in heaven also!

Although Mr. Ross had come forward, he still struggled

Along the Sawdust Trail

with that poisonous weed. He was determined never to touch it again, but that night he was really being tortured with the desire to smoke. As he paced the floor of their little cabin, suddenly he heard a knock at the door. It was the preacher.

"I just thought I would stop by and see how you were doing," the minister said.

"I knew you would come, I just knew you would come," Mr. Ross exclaimed over and over.

There was half-a-pack of cigarettes on the table. "Better throw those in the stove," suggested the minister, "Then let's kneel down here to ask God to take this craving away immediately or give you strength to fight it through."

Mr. Ross agreed to pray, and as they knelt together, his prayer was simple: "Lord, make me clean."

The preacher went on his way, but the next evening he stopped by again. This time it was different. Mr. Ross was master of the situation and with a smile he said, "The tobacco is gone. Today I was working with a man who was smoking, and I told him it smelled like old burnt rags." Again the preacher knelt with Mr. Ross as together they thanked God for the victory.

Soon the Rosses were baptized and became members of the Seventh-day Adventist Church. They witnessed for their Master at every opportunity. Whenever Mr. Ross met any of his old friends, he spoke of his church. His changed life testified to everyone of the wonderful power of God, through whose grace he had been transformed.

The Rosses have been dead for many years now. They are buried in a cemetery in The Dalles, Oregon, but we look forward to seeing them again someday in the earth made new.

CHAPTER THREE

The Way of the Transgressor Is Hard

◆ ◆ ◆

The Evangelistic Trail became rugged now, and shadows crossed its path. Not everyone who heard the Spirit's call responded to the invitation. From The Dalles, the tabernacle was moved to Eugene, Oregon, and we prayed earnestly that God would speak through lips of clay to the inhabitants of this beautiful university city.

People became curious as they read the sign in front of the tabernacle. "*Venden Brothers. Back to the Bible. Bring Yours.*" On entering, they saw in back of the pulpit a banner that displayed the words, "*What Shall It Profit A Man, If He Shall Gain The Whole World, And Lose His Own Soul?*" (Mark 8:36). That was a sermon in itself, and it is a good question for each one of us to consider!

People came night after night, and many took their

Along the Sawdust Trail

stand on the Lord's side, but I especially remember one couple. They heard a sermon entitled "How the Whole World Went Astray on a Great Vital Truth" (see p, 105). This sermon dealt with the importance of God's law, including observance of the seventh-day Sabbath rather than worshiping on Sunday, the first day of the week.

This was a test and called for some serious reflection. Satan was on hand to discourage and cause doubts in the minds of the people. The great controversy, which had been going on for over six thousand years, was particularly apparent that night.

One particular couple was having a real battle with the enemy of souls. The husband had a good job with the county, which he felt he could not give up to keep the Sabbath. He heard the beautiful words of the hymn, "All to Jesus, I Freely Give," but he hardened his heart and let Satan take control. He never came to the tabernacle again, but the next Sabbath his wife left home to go to church. She went a few blocks and then turned back, feeling she couldn't go without her husband.

Soon, because of the Depression, her husband lost his job. He became moody and sad. He had hardened his heart and rejected the pleading of the Holy Spirit. One morning as his wife was preparing breakfast, he went outside. She called him to breakfast, but he didn't come, so she went looking for him. To her horror, she found him lying in a pool of blood in the garage. In his discouragement, he had slashed his throat and bled to death.

We were shocked when we heard the news and asked ourselves whether we had done all we could to help this poor man.

The Way of the Transgressor Is Hard

When Jesus was here on earth, traveling the Evangelistic Trail, He sometimes prayed all night. When He talked to the woman at the well, His physical needs were secondary, and He forgot that He was hungry and tired. The worth of a soul meant so much to Him that it finally led Him to Calvary.

CHAPTER FOUR

He Leadeth Me—Three Families' Experiences

"He leadeth me! O.blessed thought!
O words with heavenly comfort fraught!
Whate'er I do, wheree'er I be,
Still 'tis God's hand that leadeth me."

Mrs. Wheeler

When we were in Medford, Oregon, a Catholic woman from Minnesota—a Mrs. Wheeler—came to visit her daughter whom she had not seen for a number of years. She was surprised to find her daughter divorced from her husband and living a very worldly life with another man. This made Mrs. Wheeler very sad, so she went to the priest and poured out her heart to him. He told her that she had better go back to her home and not meddle

Along the Sawdust Trail

with her daughter's affairs.

Somehow through God's leading, an Adventist woman came in contact with Mrs. Wheeler and invited her to go to the evangelistic meetings we were having.

An emphatic "No!" was her response. "I cannot go to a Protestant church. That would be sin." Her new friend told her this was not a church but a public building where all were welcome, regardless of their religion. She added that the music and song was so beautiful, she should come just to enjoy it. And she did!

She loved the music, but as soon as the sermon began, she dropped her head and tried not to listen. When she got home she said the rosary and decided not to go again. She went to her priest and confessed her sins. The priest insisted that she leave for her home in St. Paul immediately, but the Holy Spirit answered the prayers of God's people and brought her back to the tabernacle. Her faith in the Catholic Church was being shaken, but the new truths she had been hearing seemed unclear. She became discouraged and again stopped coming to the meetings.

Because our boys were so young at that time, I did not attend all of the lectures. On one of the evenings I stayed home, I answered a knock at my door and discovered Mrs. Wheeler. We visited together until my husband came home. She told him that she had lost some of her faith in the Catholic Church and in the rosary which had meant so much to her through the years. Now she felt she had nothing and didn't know how to pray. My husband told her that she could talk to God as to a friend and put her burdens on the Lord, who hears every sincere prayer. Melvin prayed earnestly for her.

The next morning she called us to tell us of a happy experience. That night she had knelt by her bed and talked to God as Melvin had told her she could. A great peace came into her heart, and she went to sleep. In the night she awakened, and her room was full of light! It seemed that the very presence of God was there. The love of Jesus filled her heart, and she made a decision to follow Him and keep all of His commandments. Another captive had been rescued for God's kingdom.

She is sleeping now, awaiting the call of the Life-Giver. What a joy it will be to see Mrs. Wheeler again someday.

The Whites

The White family was living in Canada when a terrible lightning storm blew the lights out in their house. The father called to each member of the family. All but two of the boys answered. With flashlight in hand, he went to find them. Much to the family's sorrow, he found that they had been struck by the lightning and were both dead.

Deciding to sell everything, the father, mother, two daughters, and one son packed and moved to Ohio, leaving two lonely graves behind in Canada. Some time later, they moved again, this time to Washington. When they arrived in Spokane, they developed some car trouble and had to stay over a few days.

It happened that one of the evangelists was holding meetings there. Mr. White noticed in the paper what the subject was for the evening lecture and suggested that the family go to hear this preacher. The wonderful message they heard brought comfort and courage to their sorrowing hearts. Wanting to hear more, they stayed in Spokane and went night after night to listen to the wonderful words of life. At the close of the series, Mr. and Mrs. White were baptized, and they moved on to Portland, Oregon.

A number of years later, when the Venden brothers held a crusade in Portland, they attended those meetings as well, and told us the story leading up to their conversion in Spokane. God works in marvelous ways His wonders to perform.

The Robinsons

In Salem, Oregon, Mr. and Mrs. Robinson, along with their sixteen-year old son, were present at the tabernacle almost every night. Near the end of the series was a sermon entitled "*Weighed in the Balance and Found Wanting*," which was about the feast of Belshazzar and the handwriting on the wall.

At the feast, Belshazzar and a thousand of his lords drank from the Hebrew temple's golden vessels. In the night, as they reveled in the royal palace hall, they were seized with consternation as a bloodless hand appeared and began writing upon the wall.

At the close of the meeting, an appeal was made for all to come forward who wanted to be on the Lord's side. The Robinsons made no move. As they walked home, no one spoke a word. They retired for the night, but their son could not sleep. He came to his parents' room and solemnly said, "I feel terrible. I think if we don't make a decision now, we will all be lost."

His dad was touched by the earnestness of his son

but persuaded him to go back to bed and told him they would talk things over in the morning. The clock struck two a.m., and still Robert couldn't sleep. Again he came to his parents' room and pled with them. His father got up, and they all dressed and went over to Dan Venden's home and rang the doorbell.

Dan called out, "Who is it?"

"The Robinsons," was the response. "And we have come to talk to you about our souls' salvation."

We were reminded of the story of Nicodemus who came to talk to Jesus by night. The Holy Spirit brought conviction and peace to the Robinson family that night, and a great victory was won for Christ.

> Holy Spirit, faithful Guide,
> Ever near the Christian's side,
> Gently lead us by the hand,
> Pilgrims in a desert land;
> Weary souls fore'er rejoice,
> While they hear that sweetest voice.

Mr. Robinson had an important job, and he thought he might be laid off. As he explained to those over him that he had joined the Seventh-day Adventist Church and could not work on Saturday, the company granted his request and in a few months raised his salary, proving that "all things work together for good to them that love God" (Romans 8:28).

CHAPTER FIVE

Threat of Death

◆ ◆ ◆

Every day over the radio, we hear about the sixth commandment being broken. It started way back at the beginning with Cain killing Abel. Now thousands are killed every day.

In Portland, Oregon, a big strong man wanted to kill the Venden brothers. He had no reason for this, except that he didn't want his wife and grown son, who were attending the evangelistic meetings, to become Seventh-day Adventists. But they kept on coming and after several months, they decided to be baptized. On the last Sabbath in the series, with many others, they took their stand for God's truth, regardless of the husband's serious threats. When they came home from the meeting, he asked them if they had been baptized. When they told him they had,

Along the Sawdust Trail

he flew into a rage and with his strong arm knocked them to the floor.

Nearby neighbors heard the commotion and knew of his plans to kill the Venden brothers, who had influenced his wife and son to be baptized. The enraged man started up the street toward the Venden home. These neighbors alerted the Vendens that he was coming. Dan and Nellie pulled down all the shades, locked the doors, and went into the back bedroom to pray for God's protection and for this poor man's soul.

He came and pounded on the door, shouting like a madman. Finally, after no response came from within, he went back to his home. Through the prayers of God's people a miracle happened, and this man, who had been one of Satan's captives, confessed his sins and begged forgiveness from his wife and son. He, too, was transformed through God's grace.

CHAPTER SIX

On the Trail East

One ship sails East
And one sails West
By the selfsame wind
That blows,
'Tis the set of the sail
And not the gale
That determines
The way we go.

The gale blew toward the east, and swiftly the evangelistic team traveled in that direction. They carried only a few trunks and suitcases as they departed from Portland's Central Railroad Station.

The call had come, "The large cities need to be evan-

Along the Sawdust Trail

gelized." The millions in New York City must hear about the love of God and the message of the third angel.

The Brooklyn Academy of Music was rented for a crusade. Thousands of handbills were distributed. Daily radio announcements were aired. Then the miracle happened. The auditorium was almost filled to capacity on the opening night.

New York City's residents came from all walks of life. Some came from slums, some from nobility, some were discouraged, some really wanted to know God, and some came just from idle curiosity.

The few Seventh-day Adventists in that large city shared with the evangelists a burden for the many souls who were so desperately in need of God. Only through much prayer and the working of the Holy Spirit could their lives be changed.

Bill Schultz

One night after the meeting, a man in his thirties stopped momentarily at the door and said to the speaker, "Pray for me." This happened several times. Soon the evangelist knew the man's name and where he lived. One night he asked, "Bill, what is troubling you?"

This is the story from a heart that had been touched by the mighty power of the Holy Spirit. When Bill Schultz finished college, he applied for a job in Manhattan's Hanover Bank. Because of his good personality and keen intellect, he was hired and had worked there for twelve years. He had been promoted to the responsibility of being in charge of all the securities, a job that involved managing millions of dollars.

On the Trail East

Now he had a problem. He had learned that the seventh day was the Sabbath, but Bill was expected to be at work that day. He spoke to one of his superiors regarding his convictions and told what he had learned from the evangelistic meetings. On Friday he asked to have his Sabbath off, but his request was denied, and the man answered, "What kind of crazy religion are you getting into, anyway?"

His boss, with others from the department, tried to intimidate him. At last he weakened and went to work, but the day turned out to be a miserable one. He came home that night sick. He could not eat, he ached all over, and as he lay in his bed, he was tortured with remorse.

About nine o'clock that night, the Holy Spirit impressed Melvin with the thought that Bill Schultz was in serious trouble. He responded by driving the considerable distance to Bill's home, where he found poor Bill in a sad condition.

He sat down by his bed and talked to him, but there was no response. Melvin decided to use some therapeutics. He put a cold towel on Bill's head and began to massage his limbs. As he relaxed, Bill told of the experience he had gone through that day. He said he had decided that he could not give up his job. The sacrifice was too great! He then refused to talk further.

The evangelist wondered what he could do and felt impressed by the Holy Spirit to pray. So he knelt beside that bed and prayed earnestly that God would help poor Bill in his hour of crisis. He read some of God's precious promises, revealing the marvelous love of Jesus for every human being. As Bill listened, his heart was touched. Tears of remorse were shed, and Bill prayed for forgiveness. He asked God to help him to believe His promises and be a true and faithful witness for Him.

The next Friday, the same group of men again tried to weaken his faith, but this time it was different. Bill did the talking and explained how important it was for him to obey God. He told of the peace that had come into his own heart as he had made his commitment to the Lord.

He lost his job, and his faith was really tested! For months he walked the streets looking for work, stopping at all the employment agencies. It was during the depression of the early thirties, and though the outlook was discouraging, the uplook was still good.

Bill kept on praying. In caring for his family, most of his savings were depleted, and he was completely dependent upon the Lord. But man's extremity is God's opportunity, and a miracle happened. He was offered a job in a large warehouse handling heavy equipment. The pay was far less than he had received in the Hanover Bank, but he was thankful to have work, even though he went home many nights with an aching back.

During the course of the next year, he was called to serve on a jury for a few days. At the end of that month he received his full salary as usual. He went to the warehouse superintendent and told him he had been paid for the jury duty, so that amount should be deducted from his salary. The man was amazed at his honesty. He had never been confronted with a request like that before. Bill was just the man they needed, and he was shortly promoted. Later on, he became a representative for the company and received a better salary than he had from the Hanover Bank.

God works in wondrous ways His mysteries to perform. Our heavenly Father watches over his people! As the psalm of David puts it so beautifully, "I have been young, and now am old; yet have I not seen the righteous forsaken, nor his seed begging bread" (Psalm 37:25).

And Others

There were many wealthy widows living in New York City at this time. Two of these who were sisters came to the Brooklyn Academy of Music night after night to hear what the evangelists had to say. One evening, as the speaker shook hands with them at the door, one of the sisters stated, "We are good Methodists."

To which he quickly replied, "Good Methodists make good Seventh-day Adventists." Before the meetings closed, they were baptized and one of the sisters gave the Greater New York Conference a large enough sum of money to cover the expenses of the entire crusade.

We all praised the Lord for this generous gift and were mindful of a hymn that surely expressed her sentiments:

Lord, I care not for riches,
Neither silver nor gold;
I would make sure of heaven,
I would enter the fold;
In the book of Thy kingdom,
With its pages so fair,
Tell me, Jesus, my Saviour,
Is my name written there?

One day a well-dressed man walking along the street saw a piece of paper in the gutter. He picked it up and

Along the Sawdust Trail

discovered it to be one of the cards announcing meetings being held by the Venden brothers. He was interested and came that very night. He heard the message of the third angel: *Babylon is fallen. Come out of her, My people.* He kept coming to the meetings and eventually made his decision to come out of Babylon.

Before the crusade left New York City, a large number came out of Babylon and identified with the remnant people, helping in every way they could to strengthen the work in that large city. God only knows the far-reaching influence of those dedicated people.

Someday we will stand together in the New Jerusalem with the saints of all the ages and sing praises to God the Father, Christ the Son, and the Holy Spirit for the gift of Jesus and His marvelous love demonstrated at Calvary.

CHAPTER SEVEN

The Trail to Philadelphia

♦ ♦ ♦

And to the angel of the church in Philadelphia write . . . Behold, I come quickly: hold that fast which thou hast, that no man take thy crown. Him that overcometh will I make a pillar in the temple of my God, and he shall go no more out: and I will write upon him the name of my God, and the name of the city of my God, which is New Jerusalem, which cometh down out of heaven from my God: and I will write upon him my new name (Revelation 3:7,11-12).

Philadelphia, "the City of Brotherly Love," was next to hear the gospel of the love of God as the Trail and the evangelistic team turned back toward the west. A very fine hall was secured for the Prophecy Speaks Crusade, and handbills were scattered far and wide. Announcements were made on the radio and in the newspapers.

The Hartleins

During the early part of the crusade, a mother and one daughter came almost every night. The husband, and father of that home, had recently died, leaving behind an empty chair and a desire for the hope that only God can supply.

They were particularly interested in the sermon regarding life after death. Both mother and daughter found comfort in John 11:25, where Jesus said to Martha, "I am the resurrection, and the life: he that believeth in me, though he were dead, yet shall he live." Even though the mother was comforted, her two sons would have no part in it and refused to attend any of the meetings.

It was midwinter, and much to the joy of the Hartlein boys, the ponds in the parks were frozen over. Ice skating was the one sport they loved most! It just happened to be a sport much loved by the evangelist also. As a boy, Melvin had learned to skate backwards and forwards and to cut circles. He was quite an expert skater, and he got the idea that perhaps this common link could prove useful.

So he called one day and asked the boys if they liked to skate, though he already knew the answer. When they answered Yes, he suggested that they all go skating together. They were delighted to meet him at one of the large skating ponds. Melvin's abilities on skates were greatly admired by the boys, and a lasting friendship began. This opened their hearts to him and his message, and from then on they never missed a meeting. At the close of the crusade, the whole family was baptized.

These young people became workers in the denomination. The daughter taught church school for many years, one son became the principal of a Seventh-day Adventist academy, and the other son went into construction work and built churches throughout the conference.

The last time we saw him, he was working on the Tacoma Park church. He laid down his hammer, and we visited for a few minutes, reminiscing on the crusade held in Philadelphia and on the skating experience.

In the "City of Brotherly Love," these precious ones learned of the wonderful love of Jesus.

When Jesus calls His jewels
From ev'ry land and sea,
And takes them home to glory,
What a meeting that will be!
We'll meet the friends departed,—
The loved ones called away,
Not one will be forgotten,
In that glad reunion day.

The Matterns

Mr. Mattern was a railroad station clerk. His wife was an Adventist, and when her husband had a Saturday off, now and then he would go to church with her. While attending the crusade meetings, he was impressed with the importance of keeping all of the commandments, including the fourth one.

The words on the large sign above the pulpit bothered him. The sign read: *What shall it profit a man if he shall gain*

Along the Sawdust Trail

the whole world and lose his own soul? So Mr. Mattern spoke to his boss at the station. He told him he could not work on Saturday anymore and explained the reason why. The first time he was absent on the Sabbath, the company deducted one day's wages. The next time he missed, it cost him two days wages. The third time, he lost three days wages.

Mattern was a valuable man at the station, and they didn't want to lose him, but they could not understand his peculiar ideas. They decided to call a psychologist to examine him. The psychologist found him very alert and gave a fine report to the station manager! After that, he received his Sabbaths off and was able to continue working there until he retired. He now lives in Florida, where he still witnesses for his Lord!

CHAPTER EIGHT

The Trail to Michigan

◆ ◆ ◆

The trail crossed Ohio next and swung up into Michigan. A crusade was conducted in the city of Muskegon, on the shore of Lake Michigan. Many precious souls accepted the third angel's message and took their stand with God's commandment-keeping people.

One lady and her husband became curious when they saw the announcement in the paper, *Bible Prophecy Lectures—All Are Invited.* They attended the meetings for a few nights; then the husband decided he would rather attend the theater. His wife had become interested, however, and came by herself. Her husband fumed and fussed as he saw her becoming more and more interested. Finally one night he said, "You can't be my wife and be a Seventh-day Adventist."

She stood tall and said to him, "If I can't be a Seventh-

Along the Sawdust Trail

day Adventist and be your wife, I'll be a Seventh-day Adventist and *not be* your wife."

He really loved her and decided he must be missing out on something important. The next evening he decided to go with her. Every evening after that, they attended together.

They both were baptized, and what a happy day it was! This dear lady had believed Jesus' words in Matthew 10:37; "He that loveth father or mother" (or husband) "more than me is not worthy of me: and he that loveth son or daughter more than me is not worthy of me."

Another experience, while in Muskegon, began with a phone call. When Melvin answered, a voice said, "My husband and I are elderly folks and not able to go to the evangelistic meeting, but we hear you every day on the radio. We wish so much that we could see you and talk with you." In a few days my husband called on them and began to study the Bible with them. It was just what they were searching for and before we left Muskegon, they, too, were baptized.

Now the interesting part: A niece of theirs had been attending some evangelistic meetings in Detroit. She had become a Seventh-day Adventist and had a great burden for her aunt. At the same time the aunt, unaware of what had happened in Detroit, had a burden for her niece. Shortly, the niece came to visit her aunt, hoping to tell her of her newfound faith. Each tried to be as tactful as possible while proceeding with the same mission. Soon the truth came out. They discovered that they were both members of the Seventh-day Adventist Church. With tears of joy, they rejoiced together.

"The world passeth away, and the lust thereof; but he that doeth the will of God abideth for ever" (1 John 2:17).

We thank God for this promise.

CHAPTER NINE

The Trail Leads to Grand Rapids

◆ ◆ ◆

Next, the Evangelistic Trail led us to Grand Rapids, Michigan, a beautiful city with a very fine auditorium that we hoped to rent.

When the Venden brothers told the auditorium manager that they would like to rent the auditorium for one hundred nights, he was surprised. No religious group had ever approached him with a proposition like that, and he wasn't sure he liked the idea. He quoted a price that was much too high. The team decided to appeal to the city council for a more reasonable rent on the auditorium. As the council deliberated, the evangelistic team prayed earnestly that their decision would be favorable. It was, and the building was made available for the entire time they had requested!

The building actually contained two auditoriums un-

Along the Sawdust Trail

der one roof, both of which shared the same lobby. One of the auditoriums seated 5,000, while the other accommodated 1,200. The first night's meeting was held in the smaller room.

That night the crowd was so large that many people could not get in. The sermon titled, "Where and What is Heaven," posed an important question to many thinking people, as evidenced by the crowd. In keeping with the meeting's theme, a duet sung by the Venden brothers awakened their desire to have a home in heaven at last.

I have heard of a land
In that far away strand,
In the Bible the story is told
Where no sorrow shall come,
Neither darkness nor gloom,
And nothing shall ever grow old."

At the end of the evening, it was announced that Sunday night's meeting would be held in the large auditorium. The subject would be "Seven Words of a Great Bible Prophecy That Spell Doom to Hitler." The year was 1942, and many feared that Hitler would take over all the nations of Europe. But God is in control of nations.

On Sunday night, the large auditorium was filled with people who came out and listened spellbound to the Bible prophecies explained. Most of the people in Grand Rapids belonged to the Dutch Reformed Church, and the prophecies in God's Word were foreign to them.

As the lectures continued, the evangelistic team became better acquainted with the folks who attended from night to night. The Holy Spirit was present and—as in other places—spoke through lips of clay, proclaiming the wonderful love of Jesus and His ability to change lives. The discouraged became courageous, the disappointed became hopeful, the sad became joyous, and the Christians became more like Christ.

One day a young woman named Mildred came to our home with problems. She had become convicted that she ought not to work on Saturday because it was the Sabbath of the fourth commandment. Her position as an operator at the telephone office was an important one, but her relationship with her Lord had become more important to her than anything else. We prayed with her and encouraged her to do what she felt God wanted her to do. She had already talked with the manager, and he had told her they could not comply with her wishes to avoid Saturday work. She made her decision and informed her manager that she had worked her last Saturday.

Again, a miracle happened. The next day the manager told her that she was too valuable a person for them to lose and that she could have her Sabbaths off. Mildred was not only valuable to them, but she was very precious to the Lord, and through her influence I am sure many others will be in the kingdom. Again I think of the truth that "No Man is an Island, No One Stands Alone."

When Mildred retired, the telephone company gave her a big party. At that party, they gave her permission to make free long distance calls—anywhere in the United States—for the rest of her life. Many times each year we hear her voice coming over the phone from Grand Rapids, Michigan, where she and her sister Edythe still live.

Grandpa Nels from Norway became a
Seventh-day Adventist by reading his
Bible (died at age forty-four).

Melvin and Ivy Ruth as
newlyweds.

Grandma
Christine
surrounded
by her grown
children (Nels
and two other
daughters were
deceased by
this time.)

The Venden brothers
at the dawn of their
evangelism career.

The Venden brothers at
Carnegie Hall, New York City
(1939).

Handbill
announcing
the meetings
in Grand
Rapids,
Michigan
(1941).

"The Man who came to a Wedding with a Suit Borrowed from the Penitentiary"
UN-FORGETABLE—STARTLING—TOO THRILLING FOR WORDS!
Sunday Night Dec. 28, 7:20
CIVIC AUDITORIUM
BLACK AND SILVER HALL   GRAND RAPIDS, MICHIGAN
VENDEN BROS. "SEARCHLIGHT OF PROPHECY" LECTURES
People anywhere to come for miles to attend these lectures
RADIO .... **WLAV**

THE GREATEST QUESTION
EVER ASKED IN THE HISTORY OF THE WORLD
STARTLING, NOT A DULL MOMENT — Stereopticon Pictures
Sunday Night Dec. 21, 7:15
CIVIC AUDITORIUM
BLACK AND SILVER HALL   GRAND RAPIDS, MICHIGAN
VENDEN BROS. "SEARCHLIGHT OF PROPHECY" LECTURES
RADIO .... **WLAV**

HEAR IT!
NOTHING LIKE IT EVER GIVEN BEFORE, EXCEPT THE FAMOUS THREE-HOUR SERMON OF PAUL KASHMIRI, IN WHICH HE COVERED THE ENTIRE CHRISTIAN RELIGION.
VENDEN'S
Great Three-Hour Sermon
THRILLING FROM START TO FINISH!
SUN., FEB. 1 · 7 to 10 p. m.
COME AND GO AS YOU PLEASE   YOU WON'T GO TO SLEEP
CIVIC AUDITORIUM
BLACK AND SILVER HALL   GRAND RAPIDS, MICHIGAN
LISTEN TO RADIO WLAV

Typical announcement cards that faithful church members distributed by the thousands.

Melvin (M.L.) Venden— a passion for evangelism

Well-known Adventist evangelists during the thirties and forties.

First row: Alden Owen Sage, Paul Omar Campbell, Don Hiatt Spillman, Louis K. Dickson, Charles T. Everson, Melvin L. Venden.
Second row: Henry G. Stoehr, Roy Allan Anderson, George Edward Peters, Beveridge R. Spear, Frederick F. Schwindt, Samuel G. Joyce.
Third row: Daniel E. Venden, John G. Mitchell, Carlyle B. Haynes, Clifford A. Reeves, Francis D. Nichol, John L. Shuler.

The team: Melvin, Dan, Ivy Ruth (l.), and Nellie

Melvin doing his best "Billy Sunday" impression.

Handbill announcing the meetings in Hanford, California (1952).

Dad and sons during evangelistic series in Sacramento, California (1956).

A favorite picture of Dad— the one who played ball with the boys.

The second generation of Venden brothers pick up the torch.

Father and son team up together (1970).

Melvin and Ivy Ruth
as they approach
retirement years.

The golden wedding anniversary.

Melvin and Ivy Ruth in their mid-eighties;
married more than sixty years.

CHAPTER TEN

Still Following the Trail

◆ ◆ ◆

The city of Flint, Michigan, was a very important place because of the automobile factories that supply work for so many people. A number of those factory workers came to the evangelistic meetings. When the testing truth—keeping God's commandments, including the seventh-day Sabbath—were presented, many of these people accepted these truths and lost their jobs. This caused no small struggle, but the Lord blessed the new believers, and they found other work. No one went hungry. Again the promise of Isaiah 1:19 was fulfilled, "If ye be willing and obedient, ye shall eat the good of the land."

The Fleischmans
During the crusade, a very fine couple by the name

of Andrew and Minnie Fleischman attended. For a time they seemed very interested, but they suddenly stopped coming. As we discovered, they belonged to the Lutheran Church and their minister, concerned for the way things were moving, gave them many reasons why they should not attend "those heretic meetings."

By this time, we had become close friends. One night they invited us to their home for dinner. Before we left, they very tactfully informed us that they felt they should stay with Martin Luther and the Lutheran Church and would not be coming to the auditorium anymore. We expressed our disappointment at their decision. But Melvin couldn't let them go so easily. A short time later, he stopped by to leave them the book *The Great Controversy*. He asked them to carefully read the chapter on Martin Luther, which they did. They were impressed, and soon these good folks were attending the meetings again.

Before long, they heard the lecture on baptism and were again put off by this new teaching. They missed the next meeting to go to their own church. Their pastor was very disturbed because some of his members were going to hear The Venden Brothers. That night he made some strong statements in regard to the human nature of Christ. He said that he believed if Christ were here today, He would wear a suit of clothes just like all other men, He would talk and act like other men. The pastor even suggested that Christ would probably smoke a pipe.

That was too much for the Fleischmans. They never went back to the Lutheran church again. They started coming back to the auditorium, but they were still struggling over what they should do. Satan was really giving them a bad time.

They had been contacted by an ingathering singing band and had enjoyed the singing very much. One night, the Lord gave Minnie a dream. In her dream, she heard the young people singing as they came down the street in front of her house. It sounded so beautiful that she went right out and joined the happy group and continued singing with them as they walked along. She awakened from her dream and woke up her husband to tell him all about it. That settled the issue for them, and they took their stand with God's commandment-keeping people. Minnie later became a Bible worker and helped many others turn their lives over to Jesus.

A Dying Man

About thirty miles from Flint was a small church in the country town of Otter Lake. Occasionally my husband went there to give the Sabbath sermon, and many of the members there made the trip in to our night meetings.

On the Sabbaths that we preached there, we would stop and give a ride to one dear lady and her little girl who lived a few miles out in the country. Her husband was not a Christian and didn't want to even see a preacher. One Sabbath, this lady invited us to come in and meet her husband. But as we came in the front door, he went out the back door. His wife was embarrassed, but my husband assured her that we were not offended in any way.

Not long after that experience, we had a call in the middle of the night from this man's wife. They had no

Along the Sawdust Trail

phone, but even though it was the dead of winter, she had walked through the snow to a neighbor's house to call us. Her husband had suffered a heart attack, and he wanted her to call Elder Venden.

It was one of those nights when the wind was blowing and flakes of snow were thick in the air. My husband was fighting a cold, but he had a burden for this poor soul. When he got to their home, it was evident that the man was dying. It was hard for him to sit up or lie down. With shortness of breath he said, "If you can do anything for this poor man, do it quick. I never could get it through my thick head why I need a Savior or why I should believe in Jesus. If you can explain it, do it now."

My husband pulled up a chair beside him and told him of the wonderful love of Jesus for all of us. He quoted many of the beautiful promises from God's Word, including "Him that cometh to me I will in no wise cast out" (John 6:37) and "The Spirit and the bride say, Come . . . and whosoever will, let him take the water of life freely" (Revelation 22:17).

This dying man seemed to grasp the thought and with his last struggling breath he said, "So much for so little, so much for so little."

My husband left him in God's hands and prayed as he drove back to our home that God would bless the words he had spoken.

Don Thomas

Another Adventist woman, who was a member of our Flint church, had a burden for her son-in-law, Don Thomas. She bought all the mimeographed sermons and sent them to him. He owned and operated his own newspaper business in Detroit, Michigan. As he read and studied the sermons, he was impressed with the truth that was so vividly portrayed, especially the fulfillment of the prophecies that bring this world down to the end time and the second coming of Jesus.

Up to this time, he had paid very little attention to his wife's religion, but now he spent hours in study and research. Over a period of months, he read all the sermons and was convinced of the truth. So he went to the pastor of the Detroit church and asked to be baptized. The pastor studied the points of our faith with him and honored his request for baptism.

Don joined his wife as a faithful member of the Seventh-day Adventist Church. In the course of time, he sold his newspaper business and was later called to be the head of the Public Relations Department for the Pacific Union Conference.

All that had transpired in the conversion experience of Don Thomas was unknown to us during our time in Flint. When the evangelistic meetings closed there, we moved on to another city. Some years later we moved to Fresno, California, where my husband pastored the church and also held evangelistic meetings in the city auditorium.

At that time, a union conference constituency session was held in the Fresno church, and Don Thomas was present. At the close of one of the meetings, he came to my husband and told him the thrilling story of his conversion and how my husband's printed sermons had been used in it. It was indeed a happy revelation of the marvel-

Along the Sawdust Trail

ous working of God's Holy Spirit.

Upon his retirement, Elder Ferren, who was head of the Public Relations Department for the General Conference, recommended Don Thomas as the man to take his place.

CHAPTER ELEVEN

Separation on the Trail

◆ ◆ ◆

Now the Venden brothers and their families had some decisions to make. For the education of their three daughters, Dan and Nellie felt they should settle in one place for a time. Dan accepted a call to be the pastor of the Union College church in Lincoln, Nebraska. Melvin and his family, however, continued traveling the Evangelistic Trail alone—though they were not really alone, for God always leads His dear children along. They were led next to Lansing, Michigan.

In Lansing, they were able to rent the Pruden Auditorium, right across from the State Capitol grounds. This auditorium had a seating capacity of about 1,200 people.

The coming crusade was well advertised, and again the large sign above the pulpit proclaimed in bold letters,

Along the Sawdust Trail

"What shall it profit a man, if he shall gain the whole world, and lose his own soul?" (Mark 8:36). That is a question we each need to consider every day. We live just a few short years here with sorrow and pain and disappointed hopes.

"The days of our years are threescore years and ten; and if by reason of strength they be fourscore years, yet is their strength labour and sorrow" (Psalm 90:10). To exchange an eternal life of joy and peace for this would be a bad bargain indeed.

There were people in Lansing who counted the cost! One young man who had encountered disappointed hopes exchanged the devil's bargain for God's bargain and took his stand on the Lord's side. He went to college and later became an Adventist minister.

Two young nurses who were engaged to be married became interested in God's bargain and severed their relationships with the men who had no interest in the things of eternity. It wasn't easy, but to them:

> The things of earth
> [became] strangely dim
> In the light of His
> glory and grace.

From Michigan these nurses moved to California, where they later married Adventist men and established Christian homes.

CHAPTER TWELVE

The Trail to Saginaw

◆ ◆ ◆

Saginaw, a city in the northern part of Michigan, was our next stop. Many Catholics and Lutherans lived there, but very few Adventists did.

We were able to obtain a hall for the crusade, but though we advertised the meetings in the *Saginaw News,* the attendance at first was not very good.

In Saginaw, we became acquainted with a woman named Mrs. Frost. She had a son named Jack Frost, who had died just before we arrived in town. So she lived alone.

Mrs. Frost was a kindhearted woman, always wanting to help someone in need. She heard that a woman on her street was sick and went to see if she could help. In her typical fashion, she was soon cleaning the house and cooking food. As she worked upstairs, Mrs. Frost saw a large

Along the Sawdust Trail

book lying on a stand. She picked it up and began to read. She became so interested she could hardly lay it down. The book was called *Daniel and Revelation*.

As she prepared to leave that evening, the woman wanted to pay her for her work, but Mrs. Frost refused any pay. "I would love to read that book I saw upstairs, however," she said.

"Take it with my gratitude," the woman answered. "My mother purchased it from a colporteur years ago. Mrs. Frost was delighted and sat up late reading the precious book.

She saw in the *Saginaw News* that Evangelist Venden was holding meetings in the city auditorium and wondered if he was preaching anything about what she had been reading. She came to the meetings to check him out and was amazed to find that what he said agreed with her book. Each evening when she returned home, she would read in her book, which became more and more precious to her. Finally, she made the decision to be baptized and became a member of the church. For many years, she was a faithful helper to the other members there.

One day in heaven, perhaps, she will be able to meet the faithful colporteur who left that book behind.

I must not forget to add a few words about Mae Zoraman. She accepted the truth in Grand Rapids, but since she had no relatives and lived alone, she moved right along with us whenever and wherever we went for the next series. Each evening she came early to the auditorium. She would make certain that the songbooks were placed on the chairs and help with other things as she could. When we later moved to California, she felt that she should remain in Saginaw and help in our small church there. She was a humble, dedicated Christian. She gave the rest of her life to the believers in Saginaw and finally died there. If we are faithful, I believe we will see her again.

CHAPTER THIRTEEN

California Stops Along the Trail

◆ ◆ ◆

We crossed many states before we drove into the beautiful city of Modesto, California. Modesto had just the kind of school we were looking for—a Seventh-day Adventist academy that our boys could attend. By this time, Louis was a sophomore in high school and Morris was in the eighth grade. This break from the Trail meant that our sons could attend school and still live at home.

The Lord blessed in a wonderful way as my husband pastored the church there and also held evangelistic meetings. The church members prayed earnestly, and God's Holy Spirit changed the lives of many loved ones.

Mrs. Ellis and her two children prayed for Mr. Ellis. In his work as a salesman, he often ate and drank with other businessmen. Occasionally, he would join them for an

Along the Sawdust Trail

alcoholic drink. Soon this became a habit with him, and he began drinking more and more.

One Sunday night his wife persuaded him to attend the meeting with her. The subject was The Great Judgment Day, and he saw himself in the picture. He went home that night stunned. He could not sleep, realizing that he was a lost man if he continued the way he was going. He continued attending the meetings with his wife, and through the prayers of his family and others, his life was changed. He was baptized and became a zealous worker for the Lord. As a colporteur, he was used by God to bring many souls to the kingdom.

Mr. and Mrs. Showalter came to the meetings out of curiosity. He had once belonged to another church, but when he was drafted into the army, he gave up all his beliefs and started smoking.

The first sermon they heard was on "The Mark of the Beast." Mr. Showalter was so stunned by this idea of being marked by Satan that on the way home that night he threw away his cigarettes. They returned to the meetings every night and finally decided that they must keep the Sabbath.

Having made his decision, Mr. Showalter placed a sign in his barbershop window that read "Closed on Saturday, Open on Sunday." His friends agreed that this idea would never work and that he would lose his business for certain. But the Lord blessed in a marvelous way, and he had more customers on Sunday than he had ever had on Saturday. He took an active part in the church services, and through his influence, many souls were won for Jesus.

On the Trail only one hundred miles south of Modesto, the city of Fresno had a very fine auditorium. We were able to rent it for a certain number of evenings, so meetings were scheduled to begin on a Sunday night.

Across from the auditorium, a new service station had been completed, and to draw attention to its opening that same Sunday evening, the owners had a powerful searchlight flashing back and forth across the sky. It lighted up our auditorium, as well as the large sign over the entrance that read, "*Bible Prophecy Crusade by Evangelist Melvin L. Venden.*"

We thanked the Lord for the searchlight provided by the owners of the service station and were again mindful that God works in marvelous ways, His wonders to perform.

Here are some of the many and varied experiences the believers shared as they took their stand to follow Jesus all the way.

Three sisters who lived a few miles out of town came every night to the meetings. Two or three years before, an Adventist minister had held some evangelistic meetings locally, and they had been interested. But when the minister visited their home, their father had ordered him off the place.

The father had since died, and these young women took their stand for the Sabbath truth. They were a part of the many who were baptized there.

Also in Fresno, there was an artist named Vida Booth Ellis. She came to the auditorium night after night, but she had a problem. She was a slave to cigarettes, and she was quite ashamed that she could not kick the habit. One day in despair, she came to our house in tears and told us about her problem.

My husband said, "Let's pray about it." So we knelt and earnestly prayed for the Lord to give her the victory. We arose from our knees, and Vida claimed the promise

Along the Sawdust Trail

in John 14:13, "Whatsoever ye shall ask in my name, that will I do." She never smoked again. She was baptized and became a faithful Seventh-day Adventist.

A few months later, she was at the General Conference Session in San Francisco when a call was made for a special evangelism offering. She took out her checkbook and wrote a check for four thousand dollars. Later, the Union Conference asked us to hold a campaign in Phoenix, Arizona, using part of the money she had given.

On the wall of our St. Helena, California, home, we have a large, beautiful painting by Vida Booth Ellis, which she gave to us. It is a precious reminder of a soul won for Christ and eternal life.

"Never can the cost of our redemption be realized until the redeemed shall stand with the Redeemer before the throne of God. Then as the glories of the eternal home burst upon our enraptured senses we shall remember that Jesus left all this for us, that He not only became an exile from the heavenly courts, but for us took the risk of failure and eternal loss. Then we shall cast our crowns at His feet, and raise the song, 'Worthy is the Lamb that was slain to receive power, and riches, and wisdom, and strength, and honor, and glory, and blessing' " (*The Desire of Ages, p. 131*).

Another thrilling experience involved a man who did pickup and delivery for a large laundry. He had been coming to all the meetings, though his wife had only attended a few times. She really did not understand the messages or his interest in them.

One day her husband stopped at our house. He was concerned about his job because he had made up his mind that he must keep the Sabbath. My husband quoted many of the precious promises and encouraged him to step out in faith.

His decision was further complicated when his wife told him that she would leave him if he became a Seventh-day Adventist. He was reminded of Matthew 10:37, "He that loveth father or mother more than me," (which could include one's wife also) "is not worthy of me." As the Holy Spirit spoke to his heart, he made his decision to be faithful come what may and was baptized during the next baptism.

He lost his job, but the Lord rewarded his faith with other work and better pay. His wife did leave him for a time, but she really loved him and later came back to him. Through the influence of his changed life and her more complete understanding of the gospel, she, too, was finally baptized and became a faithful member of the Fresno Seventh-day Adventist Church.

My life, my love,
I give to thee,
Thou Lamb of God,
who died for me;
O, may I ever faithful be,
My Saviour and my God!
O thou who died on Calvary,
To save my soul
and make me free,
I consecrate my life to thee,
My Saviour and my God!

How appropriate the song to all who are bound for the Promised Land!

CHAPTER FOURTEEN

To
San Francisco

◆ ◆ ◆

In the spring of 1950, we attended the World General Conference Session in San Francisco. While we were there, Elder Baker—our Central California Conference president—asked my husband if he would be interested in holding a series of evangelistic meetings in San Francisco. He felt that the local city churches needed the inspiration that meetings could bring. And some new members would give courage and strength to the work in that large city.

My husband told Elder Baker he would consider conducting the meetings if his brother Dan, who was then President of the Nebraska Conference, could join him again. Melvin knew from talking to Dan that he was interested in getting back into evangelism.

Along the Sawdust Trail

Dan was also at the General Conference Session, so Elder Baker contacted him, and he agreed to accept such a call if it were offered. The next day the secretary of the General Conference Committee read the report of the action taken: "Voted to grant Elder D. E. Venden's request to be released from his responsibilities as President of the Nebraska Conference so that he may join his brother Elder M. L. Venden in evangelism in San Francisco."

It was a joy for us to be able to travel the Evangelistic Trail together again! Before leaving San Francisco that month, we did some house hunting and investigated the auditorium possibilities.

This was a sudden move for Dan and Nellie, so they left it up to us to make another trip into San Francisco to find places to live. The Lord guided our footsteps, and we found homes to rent within walking distance of each other. By the first of September, we were moved and had secured the Masonic Temple for our first series of meetings. What a thrill it was to be together again!

Though San Francisco was not an easy place to work, we had good support from the two main churches. During our second year, the crusade was held in the War Memorial Auditorium. As these meetings progressed, a large number took their stand for the Lord and expressed their interest in honoring Him by keeping His commandments, including the seventh-day Sabbath.

Gladys Locke, who is now living in the Seventh-day Adventist Retirement Home at Yountville, California, was one who—along with her sister—attended all the meetings. Gladys was a widow. Her sister had a husband and a family who were not interested in the message, but she took her stand regardless. The Lord was with her, and she was true to her conviction. She died a few years ago, but we are confident her name is written in the Lamb's book of life.

We also met a sea captain in San Francisco named Captain Nystol. He was a tall man whose wife was a Seventh-day Adventist. She encouraged her husband to come to the meetings with her, and he did, off and on, when he was not out to sea. He loved the ocean and the faraway places and gathered relics from many lands.

During the second year, when the crusade was held in the War Memorial Auditorium, Captain Nystol came often, and along with many others, he turned his life over to Jesus at the last baptism service.

Whenever we go to San Francisco and look out over the bay at the island of Alcatraz, we think of Frank and Minnie Johnson. The federal penitentiary, where they kept the most desperate criminals, was located on Alcatraz. Frank was a guard at the prison, and they lived there on the island as did a number of other guards and traveled back and forth to the mainland by ferry.

One day they saw an ad in the newspaper about the Venden Brothers' Crusade for Christ in the War Memorial Auditorium. They were interested and decided to see what it was all about. The meetings seemed to be just what they were looking for, so they came often.

We became good friends with the Johnsons, and they invited us out to dinner on the island of Alcatraz, which was quite an experience! Being so close to those prisoners helped us to sympathize with the families who lived there all the time.

Along the Sawdust Trail

Frank and Minnie were finally baptized. They have lived for a number of years now in a small town not many miles from our home. We have visited them often and have enjoyed their friendship very much.

I must tell you about Gladys and Russell Heigh. Their lifestyle was very different before they started coming to our meetings. The things of the world became strangely dim, and gradually a tremendous change took place. They were a talented young couple and were among those who were baptized. Later, Russell became manager of our SAWS (welfare service) Warehouse in Watsonville, where he worked for a number of years. They always attended our Dorcas Federation meetings and gave inspirational talks in support of the welfare work.

We hear from them at least once a year. They are earnest, happy Christians and are glad to belong to the family of God. Together, we are looking forward to the coming of Jesus.

CHAPTER FIFTEEN

South to Hanford

♦ ♦ ♦

Our next stop was in Hanford, California. It is an interesting town, and the small church there experienced an increase in membership when we held our evangelistic crusade in Hanford's fine auditorium.

The climate was very different from the chill and fog of San Francisco. Once again, we enjoyed the warm, mild weather. Naturally, hale and hearty evangelists are unconcerned with weather. Souls won for Jesus is the burden they carry.

The usual advertisement was placed and the date set for opening night. The people came! Some came out of curiosity, and some were hungry for the bread of life.

The evangelists greeted folks at the door as they arrived. One couple introduced themselves as the Harpers.

Along the Sawdust Trail

"Well," my husband remarked, "I have read about you in the Bible. One verse speaks of 'Harpers harping with their harps.'" Our new friends must have liked that statement, because they came every night and were among those who were baptized at the end of the crusade.

In Hanford we met Mrs. Anderson, a widow. Her husband had been a Methodist minister. She was a lovely character and a real Christian. She loved to study the Bible and came to all of our meetings. Her pastor became concerned and visited her. He left her a pamphlet detailing forty reasons why she should not become a Seventh-day Adventist.

Providentially, my husband called on her later that very evening and went over all the different reasons her minister had given her.

Mrs. Anderson looked troubled and said, "Can't I be saved in the Methodist church, keeping Sunday? Look at Billy Graham and how the Lord is using him. Won't he be saved?"

My husband assured her he could not sit in judgment on Billy Graham, but she had learned some things perhaps he did not know. "You have learned the importance of keeping the Sabbath day. You have also learned about the seal of God, the mark of the beast, and the seven last plagues. Only those who have the seal of God will be protected at that time."

Mrs. Anderson thought for a few minutes and then confessed she had a problem. She said she could never be a Seventh-day Adventist.

My husband asked, "Why do you say that, Mrs. Anderson?"

"Well," she answered, "I could never give up drinking my coffee." She claimed if she did not have that, she would get a severe headache.

With sympathy, my husband explained the wonderful love of Jesus and told of the agony He went through on the cross for us. He told how Jesus even refused the vinegar that was offered to Him when He thirsted on the cross. He read Hebrews 12:1, "Wherefore seeing we also are compassed about with so great a cloud of witnesses, let us lay aside every weight."

When he had read this she said, "My coffee habit!"

He really wasn't thinking of that but was trying to help her to see what Jesus suffered to save poor lost sinners. Mrs. Anderson's heart was touched, and she said with emphasis, "I will never drink coffee again!"

They prayed earnestly together that the Lord would give her victory over her habit. Then they claimed His promise that "God . . . will not suffer you to be tempted above that ye are able; but will with the temptation also make a way to escape, that ye may be able to bear it" (1 Corinthians 10:13).

The next Sabbath morning, we met her at the church. With a smile on her face she said, "I did not drink my coffee, and I don't even have the sign of a headache."

Dear Mrs. Anderson became a Seventh-day Adventist, and many times since, we have met her at camp meeting, where she is always smiling and thanking the Lord for His power in her life.

CHAPTER SIXTEEN

The Trail to Phoenix, Arizona

◆ ◆ ◆

The Trail led us to Arizona, rightly called cactus country for its more than one hundred varieties. Some variety of cactus is in bloom during every month of the year.

Phoenix has been considered the Millionaire's City. It is a city where every prospect pleases, and only man is vile. The climate is sunny and mild, with sunsets that exceed any we have ever seen.

We were not there merely to enjoy such exquisite marvels of nature, however. The Venden brothers were traveling this Trail with a definite purpose! To make man whole was their aim, and that begins with a foundation, which is Christ Jesus. The Evangelistic Crusade for Christ would 'ere long change the lives of many people in this western city.

The auditorium we secured was spacious and beauti-

Along the Sawdust Trail

ful, and the usual advertisements were placed in newspapers. Many handbills were scattered throughout the city. The evangelistic team went into action, and as always, our church members were faithful in inviting and bringing folks to the meetings.

One evening, a pretty teenage girl caught our attention, and we noted that she was attending regularly. The evangelists became acquainted with her and found her to be a very intelligent young person who had a desire to know God as her personal friend and Savior. One evening, she brought a young man dressed in military uniform— her brother from a military base in Texas.

He had special training as an airplane mechanic, and it just happened that a big jetliner flying over Phoenix had been forced to land because of engine trouble. So Al Weed—the brother—had been called from the base to evaluate and repair the jetliner.

While in Phoenix, his sister, Shirley, brought him to a few of the meetings. He had never heard anything like those messages, and his heart responded. He longed to know more and firmly believed that jetliner had been brought down in Phoenix for a purpose.

We gave him a set of mimeographed sermons. Some time later, he was released from the military and became a Seventh-day Adventist. In the meantime, Shirley was baptized. Through her contact and influence, she was able to win her best friend for Christ. Only eternity will reveal the many others she has helped bring to Jesus. She speaks of us as her spiritual parents, and we are happy we could have a part in her conversion.

Al moved to California and married a girl from Denmark. Later, Al was killed in a car accident, but because of his close relationship with the Lord, his family and all who knew him feel certain he will be among those who will hear the sound of the trumpet and come forth in the first resurrection. What a glorious day that will be!

CHAPTER SEVENTEEN

The Trail to the Ocean

◆ ◆ ◆

The Trail finally reached the ocean, and the end was just in sight. In the town of Santa Cruz, California, many lives were changed.

Evangelistic meetings were held in the city's auditorium. Our church membership in Santa Cruz was small, but the members were loyal to the cause they loved and helped in every way they could. Those who took their stand for the Sabbath truth were very precious to that church and to God!

Mr. H. A. Sundean, a Seventh-day Adventist man of means, built his own hospital there. The staff's deep concern for its patients had an influence that could be felt throughout the city. The sick received tender loving care that was outstanding. The hospital's reputation gave pres-

Along the Sawdust Trail

tige to our work, and a number of precious souls took their stand for truth. Some even came to the meetings from surrounding areas.

Prior to our arrival, a new church had been built in Santa Cruz. Every seventh day, it was a witness to the importance of the Sabbath. God only knows how many people will be in heaven because of the faithfulness of the members there.

When the crusade closed, Dan had a call to become president of the Central California Conference. So he and Nellie left the Trail, and again we traveled alone. This time we were called to the Northern California Conference and located in Sacramento.

The most beautiful part of it all was that our two preacher sons were also called to join us. Together, we would pastor three churches and hold evangelistic meetings as time permitted.

There had been a little friction between the three churches, but now all was calm as father and sons worked together.

We were busy people there, but the evangelistic urge was in our blood. During the winter months, we held meetings in the Tuesday Club Auditorium. It was a combined crusade with three different evangelists giving the sermons from night to night. It was exciting and a real inspiration to the members of the three churches. A large number were baptized as the churches grew and prospered.

We remember so well when Dorothy Schnell became interested in the faith. She was head of home economics for the State of California and had her office in the State Capitol Building.

The Trail to the Ocean

Her first contact with our faith was through Dr. Larry Winn, one of our good Christian doctors in Sacramento. She expressed interest, so Dr. Winn referred her to my husband. We invited her to our home and spent some time going over the points of our doctrine. When the evangelistic meetings began, she came as often as possible.

As head of home economics, she did considerable traveling to attend conventions and give lectures. As she listened to the sermons, from night to night, she was convicted that this was the church she would like to join but wondered how she could keep the Sabbath and also keep her job. Many of her trips were on weekends.

Deeply perplexed, she talked to my husband. He told her if the Lord wanted her in that job, He would work things out and if not, He had something better for her. They prayed and earnestly asked the Lord to lead. A few days later, she called to tell us that she had an appointment with the head of the Department of Education for the State of California.

In plain and simple language, she told him of her convictions. She made it clear how much she appreciated working for the state, but she explained that her whole lifestyle had changed and that now she felt compelled to follow the Holy Spirit. She said she could not work from sundown Friday night to sundown Saturday night, and if they could not use her on those terms, she would have to look elsewhere for work.

Before long, she received word that they respected the stand she had taken and felt she was too valuable to lose. Her schedule would be changed to accommodate her convictions! We all praised the Lord for His goodness, and at her baptism, the head of her department came and sat on the very front pew.

Because of her responsibilities with the state Department of Education, Mrs. Schnell was one of six members on the state Accrediting Board. Consequently, her first contact with Pacific Union College came when her committee arrived on campus to check our college for state accreditation. She was so impressed with the college that she decided it was the college for her daughter to attend.

Another young lady in Sacramento was a secretary in the Capitol Building. She gave up her position in order to keep the Sabbath, but the Lord had something better in mind for her. With a government loan, she was able to go to college, where she met and married a fine young man. As far as we know, they are still living in San Jose, California.

There were others who took their stand and became members of the remnant church.

After two years our sons left to attend seminary. We remained in Sacramento for two more years pastoring the Central Church.

Because of some difficulty in the Grass Valley church, our conference president asked if we would be willing to go there. They needed an older man of experience. We were delighted with the beauty of the country, and we appreciated the loyal members who were trying to be faithful to the Lord.

We pastored that church for seven years before retiring. We now live in St. Helena, California. We are not traveling on the Evangelistic Trail anymore, but we are still evangelists, carrying on in a different way. We are thankful for the years we were able to travel the trail and for the many precious souls we expect to meet on resurrection morning. We look forward to the day when we will take off on that wonderful flight to the New Jerusalem! What a glorious day that will be!

Though the Trail ends here, we will travel it again with many, many others through the Garden of Eden restored. It will be much more beautiful than it was in the beginning. We will walk along the river of life, and we will eat the fruit of that special tree. We will build houses and inhabit them.

We shall ever feel
the freshness of the morning
and shall ever be far from its close.
(*The Great Controversy*, page 676).

"There the wide-spreading plains swell into hills of beauty, and the mountains of God rear their lofty summits. On those peaceful plains, beside those living streams, God's people, so long pilgrims and wanderers, shall find a home" (*The Great Controversy*, page 675).

EPILOGUE

In writing this book, I have told you of lives that were transformed by God's grace. In traveling the Evangelistic Trail from coast to coast, the experiences of these dear people were multiplied many times during the years of our work.

I wish to pay tribute to all who made up our evangelistic team. There were many faithful interns, Bible instructors, song leaders, and secretaries. There were those who ran the mimeograph machines and assembled sermons that were given to interested listeners. We have never forgotten all the dear church members who were so loyal in supporting our work.

Sometimes the way was rugged and the Trail a little steep. There were many prayers and sleepless nights for

Along the Sawdust Trail

struggling ones. There were serious operations and ill health, but the Lord sustained us through it all. Because of Him there was no break in the program. Seeing thousands of precious souls in the kingdom will be a reward that will more than make up for the cost.

Now our dear brother Dan and his wife Nellie have been laid to rest. They were so dedicated and gave courage when we faced the rough spots along the Trail. Someday we shall travel together again along the river of life. Oh, what a glorious day that will be!

Today our two sons with their wives, and Dan and Nellie's three daughters and their husbands, carry heavy responsibilities in the Lord's work.

We are looking to the soon return of Jesus when the things that are seen through a glass darkly will all be made plain.

Thank God for the blessed hope!

AFTERWORD

We hope this book will find its way into the hands of the many people, families and children of those families, who came to Christ during the "sawdust" trail days—East and West. We constantly meet these people who are still faithful to the gospel of Jesus and the three angels who give glory to Him.

What an awesome thought that the prayers of our loved ones who are "sleeping" are still effective, before God's throne, for us who live!

Morris L. Venden

Along the Sawdust Trail

Bible Lecture Series Sermons
The following pages are reproductions of two original sermons from the crusade series by Elder M. L. Venden.

HOW THE WHOLE WORLD WENT ASTRAY
ON A GREAT VITAL TRUTH

Evangelist M. L. Venden
Bible Lecture Series

One bright Sunday morning a little boy kissed his mother goodbye and started down the country road to Sunday School. On his way he met some playmates who urged him to go fishing with them, instead of going to Sunday School. At first Johnny refused. He said, "I have to go to Sunday School and my mother wouldn't like it if I went fishing on Sunday!" But the boys were so persistent and the temptation so strong that Johnny weakened and went fishing with the boys instead of going to Sunday School. He tried to get home at the usual time but was a little late. His mother questioned him a little and soon had the whole story of what her boy had done.

"I'll teach you not to go fishing on Sunday," said his mother. "You go up to your room and read the fourth commandment fifty times." Alone in his room, Johnny opened his Bible to Exodus the 20th chapter and read verses 8-11—the fourth commandment. "Remember the sabbath day, to keep it holy. Six days shalt thou labour, and do all thy work; But the seventh day is the sabbath of the Lord thy God: in it thou shalt not do any work, thou, nor thy son, nor thy daughter, thy manservant, nor thy maidservant, nor thy cattle, nor thy stranger that is within thy gates: for in six days

105

Along the Sawdust Trail

the Lord made heaven and earth, the sea, and all that in them is, and rested the seventh day: wherefore the Lord blessed the sabbath day, and hallowed it." He thought for a moment and then read it again. Each time he read it, he placed a mark on a piece of paper. By the time he had read the fourth commandment fifty times, Johnny had every word of it burned into his heart. "Remember the sabbath day to keep it holy. Six days shalt thou labour and do all thy work: But the seventh day is the sabbath of the Lord thy God: in it thou shalt not do any work, thou, nor thy son, nor thy daughter, thy manservant, nor thy maidservant, nor thy cattle, nor thy stranger that is within thy gates: for in six days the Lord made heaven and earth, the sea, and all that in them is, and rested on the seventh day: wherefore the Lord blessed the sabbath day, and hallowed it." Johnny was sorry for what he had done and promised his mother that he would never go fishing again on Sunday.

Some weeks later in school Johnny's teacher happened to ask him to name the days of the week. Johnny gladly responded and said, "Monday, Tuesday, Wednesday, Thursday, Friday, Saturday, Sunday." The teacher said, "That was fine Johnny, but you started with the wrong day. You, started with Monday, the second day of the week and ended with Sunday. Sunday is the first day of the week, and not the seventh day. Saturday is the seventh day. Now you say them again, and start with the first day of the week. Johnny began by saying, "Monday, Tuesday, Wednesday, Thursday, Friday, Saturday, Sunday." The teacher said, "Johnny, I want you to do as I told you." With tears in his eyes Johnny said, "Teacher, if you had read the fourth commandment as many times as I did you would know that Sunday is the seventh day, and that God asks us to keep it holy." The teacher showed Johnny a calendar and how that Sunday is always listed on the calendar as the first day of the week. She also told him that our calendar today is the same calendar as was used in the days of Christ and that Sunday has always been the first day of the week and Saturday the seventh. That afternoon, when school was out, Johnny hur-

How the Whole World Went Astray . . .

ried home to his mother to tell her of his predicament and to find out her answer to it all. He hoped that his mother would be able to clear it all up for him.

The question as to why the large part of the professed Christian world keeps the first day of the week when the Bible commands us to keep the seventh day has perplexed most every thinking person some time. Some have thought that perhaps the calendar has been changed or that time has been lost; but such is not the case. No one ever heard of even a single family forgetting the day of the week. How could a whole nation, or the whole world, lose a day? Our present calendar of twelve months with 365 days to the year and 366 days on leap years dates back to Julius Caesar who lived before Christ. The weekly cycle has never been changed. We have an extra day in the calendar every fourth year, or leap year, which is February 29, but that in no way changes the weekly cycle. Our calendar today is the same as that used in the days of Christ.

Four years ago I had the privilege of traveling in Palestine. I shall never forget the feelings that came to me as we visited the very places where Jesus lived and labored during his earthly life. When we were in the beautiful little city of Nazareth located in the hill country of Galilee, I thought of how Jesus, the Son of God, lived there for nearly 30 years. If you and I could have lived in Nazareth in the days when Jesus was living there, I'm sure it would have been interesting to have visited His carpenter shop and to have seen Him working at His trade as a master craftsman. Day after day we might visit His shop and find Him skillfully plying His trade. But if we should chance to pass by the shop on the seventh day of the week, we would find it closed and everything quiet within. We might wonder why He had left His work; but should we follow the crowds to the beautiful synagogue in Nazareth we would find Him there, dressed in his best attire, His face radiant with a heavenly light; for He never failed to present Himself at the House of God on the Sabbath day.

All through His earthly life, Jesus manifested a very tender

Along the Sawdust Trail

regard for the Sabbath. In Luke 4:16, 22, we read these words, "And he came to Nazareth, where he had been brought up: and, as his custom was, he went into the synagogue on the sabbath day, and stood up for to read. And all bare him witness, and wondered at the gracious words which proceeded out of his mouth." Before the years of His ministry, as well as during the years of His public labors, it was His custom to go to the house of worship on the Sabbath day. Many of His greatest miracles were performed on the Sabbath. The Pharisees, who were the religious leaders of His day, had made the Sabbath a burden, and they accused Christ of breaking the Sabbath when He healed the people. But Jesus said to them, "It is lawful to do well on the sabbath days" (Matthew 12:12). The devil had worked through the Pharisees to make the Sabbath a burden. Christ showed and taught that the Sabbath was made to be a blessing, even as the commandment says, "Wherefore the Lord blessed the Sabbath day, and hallowed it."

In Mark 2:27, 28, we read how that Jesus said to the Pharisees, "The sabbath was made for man, and not man for the sabbath: therefore the Son of Man is Lord also of the sabbath." In other words, the Sabbath was made to be a blessing to man.

Did you ever wonder why Jesus said He is Lord of the Sabbath? He is Lord of the Sabbath because He made it. He is the one who is responsible for its existence. He is the one who created all things. I will prove it to you. John 1:10 says, "He was in the world, and the world was made by him, and the world knew him not." And in Hebrews 1:1, 2, we read, "God . . . hath in these last days spoken unto us by his Son, whom he hath appointed heir of all things, by whom also he made the worlds." Jesus prayed, "And now, O Father, glorify thou me with thine own self with the glory which I had with thee before the world was" (John 17:5). And in Colossians 1:13-16, it says speaking of Christ, "For by Him were all things created that are in heaven and earth."

Ephesians 3:9 says, "God created all things by Jesus Christ." It was Christ, who with His Father made everything in the beginning. It was Christ who spoke the worlds into existence. That is

How the Whole World Went Astray . . .

why, when He was here in this world, He could speak to the winds and the waves and they obeyed His voice. He could speak the word that raised the dead to life.

It was Christ who created everything in this world in six days and then rested the seventh day and blessed it and made it holy. That is why He is the Lord of the Sabbath. In Matthew 12:8 He says, "The Son of Man is Lord *even* of the sabbath day"(emphasis supplied). That little word *even* is full of meaning. If a rich man, in telling of his possessions should say, "I own that large office building, and even that great ocean liner in the harbor belongs to me," the word even would show that he considered the ocean liner his choice possession. So Jesus says, "I am Lord of heaven and earth. I made it all. I made the Sabbath day. It is the sign of My creative power, 'For in six days I, the Lord, made heaven and earth and rested the seventh day wherefore, I, the Lord, blessed the Sabbath day and hallowed it. I am Lord of heaven and earth. I am Lord *even* of the Sabbath day." We often hear Sunday called the Lord's Day. In Revelation 1:10, John says, "I was in the Spirit on the Lord's day;" and some would teach that John here referred to Sunday. But nowhere in the Scriptures is Sunday called the Lord's day. That is wholly a man-made idea. Christ claims to be Lord of the Sabbath day, so the Sabbath is the Lord's day. And the commandment says, "The seventh day is the Sabbath of the Lord thy God." And in Isaiah 58:13, the Lord calls the Sabbath "my holy day."

People often ask, "Where in the New Testament are we asked to keep the Sabbath?" I say that right here in this Scripture, in Mark 2:27, 28, the Lord says that He made the Sabbath for man. What further command do we want? If a man who is a tailor should make a beautiful suit for his little boy and then present it to him, what would you think if the boy would take the suit and tramp it in the mud? The father, who made the suit and put a lot of time and love into it, would have something to say about how the boy should treat the suit after it was given to him. Christ made the Sabbath for man to be a blessing to man. He fills it with His own love and blessing. He sanctifies it with His presence. It is a sign and memorial of His creative power. "The Sabbath was made for man." What further command could we ask?

Now since Christ made the Sabbath, He is the one who can best tell us for whom it was made. He says it was made for man. It was made at Creation and given to Adam when Adam was the only man. Some say that the Sabbath was made for the Jews. Let me ask you, Was Adam a Jew? No, there were no Jews until 2500 years after the Sabbath was given to Adam. But some would have it that the Sabbath was made for the Jews. Can you imagine that the Lord made the Sabbath at Creation and then waited for 2500 years for the Jews to come along and then picked the Sabbath up, after it had been tramped in the dust for all those centuries, and gave it to the Jews saying, "Here, I made the Sabbath back there at Creation for you?"

No, the Sabbath was made before sin ever entered. It has no thought of Jew or Gentile attached to it. The Sabbath was not made as a part of the Old Covenant or of the New, for covenants were not needed until after the Fall. It was not a shadow of the cross and the death of Christ, for then there would have been a shadow of death cast across the beautiful Garden of Eden before sin and death ever came.

The Sabbath has nothing especially in common with the Jew, for before racial divisions were thought of, the Sabbath was observed in Eden by man in his sinless state, and when the earth shall return to its Edenic beauty and perfection at the return of Christ and the setting up of His everlasting Kingdom, the Sabbath will be kept by all the redeemed. For we read in Isaiah 66:22, 23, "For as the new heavens and the new earth, which I will make, shall remain before me, saith the Lord, so shall your seed and your name remain. And it shall come to pass, that . . . from one Sabbath to another, shall all flesh come to worship before me, saith the Lord." If man had never sinned, the Sabbath would have always been kept. And the Lord declares that all flesh will come to worship before Him on the Sabbath day in the earth made

How the Whole World Went Astray . . .

new. No matter what day you observe now, dear friends, when you get to heaven, you will surely keep the Sabbath of the fourth commandment. There will be no divided heaven, half keeping the Sabbath and half keeping Sunday, but all will keep the day that Jesus sanctified and blessed at Creation. All will keep the day that the King of kings claims as His own. And I am of the opinion that if you ever keep the Sabbath over yonder, it will be well to start keeping it now.

The Sabbath has a universal and eternal reason for its existence. God blessed it and sanctified it and set it apart as a memorial of His creative power. Man is to keep it holy, for in six days the Lord made heaven and earth. The Sabbath is the birthday of Creation. And the fact that the seventh day is the Sabbath can no more be changed than your birthday can be changed. As long as Creation stands, so long will the seventh day be the Sabbath. The Sabbath is not an institution that can be transferred from one day to another. The Sabbath is the seventh day. Some people say, "We keep every day holy." But God only can make a day holy. And the only day that He made holy is the seventh day. No one can keep a day holy that God never made holy. While the Sabbath has 24 hours like the other six days, it is different because of God's blessing and because of what it stands for. Let me illustrate. If I should take a piece of linen cloth and throw it down and tramp upon it, you would have nothing to say about it. But if I should take the same kind of cloth that has been made into the United States flag and tramp it into the mud, it would be altogether a different matter. Why? Because it stands for something. By the flag we show our love and allegiance for our country. We sing, "And the Star Spangled Banner, O long may it wave; o'er the land of the free and the home of the brave."

Listen, dear friends, the seventh day Sabbath is God's flag. He says it is a sign forever that He is our God and we are His people and that He created everything in six days and rested the seventh day. He asks us to show our allegiance to our Creator by keeping holy the day that He has set apart in honor of His created works and power. There is a lot of glory and honor belonging to the One who has the wisdom and power to create worlds and suns and systems and to uphold them all in their appointed path as they speed through the universe. This world upon which we live is 25,000 miles in circumference; and it travels at a speed of 1100 miles a minute on its journey around the sun, making the trip in 365 days five hours and forty-six seconds, year after year, without losing a single second. At the same time it turns on its axis giving us day and night. Then think of the power of the Creator as revealed in the beauties and wonders of nature in plants and flowers, in fruits and grains, and vegetables for food for man and beast. Behold His wisdom in the creation of the animal kingdom. Listen to the lovely songs of the birds that gladden the heart of man. How the great Creator must have loved the things He made. Then as His crowning act of Creation He made man in His own image with a brain that could think God's thoughts after Him and appreciate and love his Creator who loved His creatures with such deep and wonderful love. Then as a tie to bind His earthly children forever to Himself in love, He made the wonderful Sabbath day for a blessing to man, that man might have one day in seven when he might forget everything else and enjoy the beauties of the handiwork of God and hold communion with His Maker on the special day appointed by the Creator Himself.

No wonder God's enemy, the devil, determined to spoil it all if he could. That's why the prophecy in Daniel, the seventh chapter, foretold that a power would arise that would presume to change God's law, and the times in the law, which is none other than the Sabbath of the fourth commandment. "And he shall speak great words against the Most High, and shall wear out the saints of the Most High, and think to change times and laws . . ." (Daniel 7:25). The devil said to himself, "I'll work to change God's law. I'll get men to turn away from their Creator and give their allegiance to me. I'll get them to keep a different day and cause them to trample on the day that God has blessed. Thus I will rob the Creator of the glory that belongs to Him as the Creator.

How the Whole World Went Astray . . .

When we were holding meetings in one of the cities on the West Coast, I noticed one day an announcement in the paper by one of the ministers of the city stating that he would speak on the subject of Why I keep the first day of the week." So the next Sunday morning I was there to hear him. The point that he emphasized in his sermon was this (and he said it with a great deal of emphasis) "God only made one Sabbath, and that is the seventh day. Sunday is not the Sabbath and Sunday school is not Sabbath school." And then to show his feelings toward the Sabbath, he said, "It makes my blood boil to hear anyone call Sunday school, Sabbath school." Then he went on to say, "If you want to keep the Sabbath you will have to keep the seventh day, for God only made one Sabbath and that is the seventh day. Go ahead and keep it if you want to, but remember when you keep the Sabbath you are keeping the gloomiest day the world ever saw. Why, the Sabbath is the day when our Lord was dead and in the tomb. Christ lay in the tomb over the hours of the Sabbath. What a dark and gloomy day that was when our Lord was dead. So, when you keep the Sabbath you are keeping the darkest and gloomiest day the world ever saw. Keep it if you want to, but I am going to keep the first day of the week in honor of Christ's resurrection. Think what a glorious day the first day of the week is. That is the day our Lord arose from the dead. While there is no command in the Bible for us to keep it; I still prefer to keep the first day of the week in honor of Christ's resurrection."

As I sat and listened I thought to myself, "That, no doubt, sounds like pretty good reasoning to someone who has never studied their Bible to know what God says about it." You know, dear friend, it is one thing to take what God has to say about a question and another thing to take what man has to say. In Proverbs 16:25 it says: "There is a way that seemeth right unto a man, but the end thereof are the ways of death." And Jesus Himself says in Matthew 15:9, "But in vain they do worship me, teaching for doctrines the commandments of men." It is one thing to see things as man sees them. It is another thing to see things as God sees them.

Along the Sawdust Trail

Now, why did Christ lay in the tomb over the Sabbath? Ah! My friend, it was not a happenstance or an accident that Christ was crucified on Friday then lay in the tomb over the Sabbath and rose from the dead on the first day of the week. Oh! No! But it was so planned in the councils of God centuries before that Christ's death should take place on Friday and that Christ should rest in the grave over the hours of the Sabbath. Why didn't He die on Monday or Wednesday or some other day of the week? Because there was a great purpose in His resting in the tomb over the Sabbath, and prophecy had foretold, centuries before, the very year that Christ was to die.

Christ died as the great Passover Lamb on the very day that the Passover lamb was slain. For fifteen centuries the Passover lamb had been slain and the service celebrated each year, and the Passover lamb had been slain on the 14th day of the month as God had directed. Every year when the Passover lamb was slain on the fourteenth day of the month, it prefigured the death of Christ who was to die as the Lamb of God. At last the year came when Christ, the real Passover was to die; and that year had been pointed out in prophecy five centuries before by the angel Gabriel to the prophet Daniel. In the ninth chapter of Daniel we read the story of how the angel Gabriel revealed to Daniel that the Messiah would cause the sacrifices to cease in the year A.D. 31 When Christ died on the cross the sacrifices ended. The sacrifices pointed forward to Christ's death, and therefore ended when Christ died. And Christ died on the cross in that very year—A.D. 31, on the fourteenth day of the first Jewish month, the very day and month on which, for fifteen long centuries, the Passover lamb had been slain.

Thus we see that the great event of all time, the death of Christ on the cross by which our salvation was purchased, was timed to the very year and month and day so that Christ would die on Friday and rest in the tomb over the sacred hours of the Sabbath. In the beginning, after finishing the work of Creation, Christ had made the Sabbath by resting on the seventh day, blessing it, making it holy, and setting it apart as a sign and memorial of his creative power and authority.

Christ was Lord of the Sabbath because he had made it in the beginning, after finishing the work of Creation. All through His earthly life He had cherished it and kept it holy. And He showed that the Sabbath was made for man, to be a blessing, even as He had blessed it in the beginning and made it holy. Even in His death He honored the Sabbath. As He had rested on the Sabbath after He had finished the work of Creation, even so He rested from His work, over the Sabbath, after He had finished the great work of redemption; thus making it a double memorial of both His creative power and His redeeming power. Was that a gloomy day when Christ lay in the tomb over the Sabbath? O! No! Not in heaven, not to God and the angels. That was the most glorious day the universe had ever seen. Why? Because all the sufferings of the dear Son of God were past and the plan of salvation had been made sure. Glorious was the future now. God and the angels rested in the Glory Land as Christ rested in the tomb over the Sabbath. There was joy in heaven because God and the angels saw the results of Christ's work. A restored creation, a redeemed race, that having conquered sin could never fall, this, the result to flow from Christ's completed work, God and the angels saw.

For four thousand years all heaven had anxiously looked forward to the awful day when the spotless Son of God would take the sinner's place and suffer the agonies of that awful death with the sins of the world crushing out His life. At last the awful day came. All heaven looked on with grief and amazement that Thursday night as Jesus agonized in the Garden of Gethsemane until He sweat great drops of blood. As He took the sinner's place that night, His Father had to withdraw His presence from Him, for "He was numbered with the transgressors" (Isaiah 53:12). The awfulness of sin and the loss of His Father's presence broke the heart of the Son of God. Christ had never sinned, and there was no reason for Him to die except as He took the sinner's place. He could have wiped the bloody sweat from His brow and gone back to heaven. His great enemy, the devil, tried to make it so hard that Christ would give up and let man perish. All heaven looked on in anxiety as Christ endured the awful suffering in Gethsemane, the shameful abuse in Pilot's judgment hall, and the agonies on Calvary 's cross. Would He endure it all and die a victor, or would He give up and let the sinners perish?

When, at last, Jesus had gone through those long hours of superhuman agony and had paid the awful price for man's redemption, He cried out, "It is finished." Then He dropped His head and died. What was finished? The great plan of redemption was finished and salvation was made sure. The death knell of Satan was rung. Christ died a victor, and throughout God's great universe there was a mighty shout of victory. In Revelation 12:10,12, we are told of the rejoicing in heaven when Christ died a victor: "And I heard a loud voice saying in heaven, Now is come salvation, and strength, and the kingdom of our God, and the power of His Christ: for the accuser of our brethren is cast down . . . . Therefore rejoice ye heavens and ye that dwell in them." All of Satan's accusations were proven false by the death of Christ, and he was conquered then and there. On the cross Christ purchased the right before the universe to destroy the devil. (See Hebrews 2:14.) And soon he will be destroyed, never to be anymore (Revelation 20).

When the disciples took Jesus down from the cross, the sun was lowering in the western sky. Tenderly they carried the bruised and mangled body of their crucified Lord down from Calvary's hill and around to Joseph's new tomb. There they gently and lovingly laid Him to rest, and as the setting of the sun ushered in the sacred hours of the Sabbath day, the Son of God rested in quietude in Joseph's tomb. The long day of shame and torture was ended, and at last He was at rest. His work completed, His hands folded in peace, He rested through the sacred hours of the Sabbath—the day that He had blessed. Thus He made the Sabbath a sign and memorial of His death for us and of His power to redeem us. When we keep the Sabbath and rest on His holy day,

How the Whole World Went Astray . . .

we show our love and loyalty to Him who is both our Creator and Redeemer.

Again, let me say that the Sabbath, when Christ rested in the tomb, was the most glorious day the universe had ever seen. There was no anxiety in the hearts of the angels or God about whether Christ would rise again. I suppose about the easiest thing the Father in heaven ever did was to call forth His Son from the tomb. For God to raise His Son back to life was no surprise to the angels, for they understood God's creative power. But, what causes the angels to marvel is how the Son of God could go through the agonies of dying in the sinner's place to save lost sinners from eternal ruin and death.

It is to the death of Christ that we owe our salvation and not to His resurrection. Throughout the eternal ages the redeemed and the angels will praise Him for His wonderful love in dying for poor lost sinners that they might live. The revelator says in Revelation 5:11, "And I beheld, and I heard the voice of many angels round about the throne . . . saying with a loud voice, Worthy is the Lamb that was slain to receive power and riches, and wisdom, and honor, and glory, and blessing." When the devil and sin and all that goes with sin is destroyed and when God makes all things new, the redeemed will ever remember how Christ died that they might live and how He rested in the tomb over the sacred hours of the Sabbath. And throughout eternity the Sabbath will ever remain a memorial of the fact that Christ created man in the beginning and that He died to redeem him.

WHY DID GOD WITHHOLD MODERN SCIENTIFIC DISCOVERIES UNTIL OUR DAY?

Evangelist M. L. Venden
Bible Lecture Series

A few years ago, we had a great Century of Progress Exposition, the 1933 Chicago World's Fair, commemorating 100 years of progress. Those of you who had the privilege of visiting that fair will remember that one of the outstanding features of that fair was the displaying of the scientific progress made during the century from 1833 to 1933. In wonderful contrast, we saw displayed how men do things today compared to the way people did the same things a hundred years ago and before. How the housewife does her work today compared to the way it was done 100 years ago. How the farmer does his work today compared to the way it was done 100 years ago. How men travel today compared to the way they traveled 100 years ago. One hundred years of increase in scientific knowledge and development.

Did you ever wonder, my friend, why and how it was that this world went on in the same old way for nearly six thousand years and then all at once everything took one sudden change? Why, for century after century down through the ages, men rubbed sticks together to make a fire or borrowed fire from their neighbors. For centuries candles were the only light used. Men reaped their grain fields by hand in the same old way for thousands of years. Women spun their yarn and wove their cloth by hand. Men traveled by sailboat or oxcart or horseback for millenniums. All the books had to be written by hand. But now, we find ourselves in a different world entirely, and the great change has taken place in one short century; in the lifetime of people that are living today.

Turn with me to a great prophecy in the Bible written 2,500 years ago. It is found in the book of Daniel. "But thou, O Daniel, shut up the words, and seal the book, even to the time of the end: many shall run to and fro, and knowledge shall be increased." Daniel 12:4. The angel Gabriel, after giving to the prophet the wonderful lines of prophecy in the book of Daniel, said, "But thou, O Daniel, shut up the words, and seal the book, even to the time *of the end*; many shall run to and fro, and knowledge shall be increased."

The prophecies of the book of Daniel were to be sealed up or not understood until the time *of the end*. When the time of the end should be reached, then the seal was to be taken off and the prophecies were to be understood. And when the time of the end should come, knowledge would be increased and men would run to and fro. Are men running to and fro today? Absolutely. Is knowledge increased? Yes, we have had a century of progress or increase of scientific knowledge. Are we living in the time of the end, spoken of by the angel Gabriel to the prophet Daniel? Yes, beyond the shadow of a doubt the last century and a little more has been the time of the end. Did the prophet know what he was talking about? Does the Bible foretell the future? Is it the Word of the Living God? A thousand times, yes.

Again we turn to another astonishing prophecy in the Old Testament written over 2,500 years ago and recorded in the book of Nahum. "The chariots shall be with flaming torches in the day of his preparation and . . . the chariots shall rage in the streets, they shall jostle one against another in the broad ways: they shall seem like torches, they shall run like the lightnings." Just think of living 2,500 years ago, in the days when on horseback or oxcart people did well to travel 20 to 30 miles in a whole day—think of a man living in such a time and saying that the time would come when the chariots would run like the lightning. To my mind, here is a prophecy that startles everybody and thrills them with confidence in the Bible as being the Word of God.

No doubt the prophet in holy vision was given a view of a modern city with the chariots or automobiles, with their headlights gleaming, running in every direction. He saw a modern traffic scene at night, and he described it in the language of his day. The things that impressed him were the torches or lights of the chariots, the chariots raging in the streets and jostling one against another in the broad ways. That sounds as though the prophet was given a view of the traffic in New York City, doesn't it? That's exactly the way it impresses you when you come into the city for the first time. And then he was impressed with the speed and he described it by saying, "They shall run like the lightning."

Now, you know, there was no need for lights on the chariots in the horse and buggy days. A horse can see the road no matter how dark it is. When I was a boy, men took more pride in their beautiful horses than people do in their automobiles today. I can remember when as a lad I rode with my father as we came home from town after dark. It was so dark that we couldn't see a thing, but we didn't bother with a light, for the horses could see, and when the horses stopped at the gate, we knew we were home. And so it had been all down through the history of the world.

But the prophet foretold that the time would come when the chariots would run like the lightning and, therefore, would have to have lights on them. Is the Bible true? Absolutely. If you don't believe it, just try driving your car on the highway at night without a light and see how long it will be until the traffic officer has you.

Why was it that the world slept on as far as scientific knowledge was concerned, for thousands of years, and then suddenly it awoke as from a long sleep? Ah, it awoke when we reached the

Along the Sawdust Trail

time of the end. As shown in other prophecies, the time of the end began with the dawn of the nineteenth century. And since the year 1798 modern inventions and discoveries have come rolling on apace. A little over a century ago people knew nothing of our modern inventions and modern ways of travel. Were they to be raised from the dead, they would be as much astonished at all those things as would the people of four thousand years ago.

In the year 1798 the balloon was invented, and since that year one great discovery after another has been made. Just notice this list as an illustration of the progress since that year:

1798	Gas for lighting purposes	1862	Monitor War Ship
1800	Cast Iron Plow	1868	Typewriter
1803	Steel Pen	1872	Automatic Airbrake
1807	Steamboat	1876	Telephone
1811	Steam Printing Press	1877	Phonograph
1818	Revolver	1879	Electric Railway
1825	Railroad Cars	1880	Seismograph
1829	Lucifer Match	1885	Linotype
1833	Reaper and Mower	1888	Steamturbine
1837	Electric Telegraph	1895	Xray
1837	Electrotyping	1895	Wireless Telegraphy
1839	Photography	1895	Motion Pictures
1846	Sewing Machine	1896	Monotype
1846	Anesthesia by Ether	1902	Radium
1851	Submarine Cable	1903	Aeroplane
1861	Gattling Gun		

And since that time, there has been the marvelous perfecting of all these inventions just named, with hundreds of new inventions in just the last few years. All of these great inventions took place since the year 1798. Go back before that time, and we find the world about where it was in the days of the patriarchs four and five thousand years ago. For thousands of years there seemed to be scarcely any advancement or improvement in knowledge.

Why Did God Withhold . . .

But suddenly with the opening of the nineteenth century, the world awoke from its long sleep and a new era dawned—the time of the end, when knowledge was to be increased.

Is it because men suddenly got better brains that we have had all those scientific discoveries? No, in the centuries of the past lived the keenest minds that the world has ever produced. Men today marvel at the literary genius and philosophical powers of men who lived over two thousand years ago. The great works of art produced by the masters of the long ago still cause the world to wonder at their achievements. Then why didn't man discover these scientific wonders before? Simply because God withheld their discovery until the time of the end. Why did He withhold them? I will tell you a little later.

Since the beginning of time, man had seen steam rise from boiling water but never discovered its great power. But when we reach the *time of the end,* the time when the world was to *speed up,* we find a man one day looking at a teakettle of boiling water. And as he saw the cover of that teakettle bobbing up and down as the steam escaped, a voice seemed to say to him, "Do you see that teakettle? There is power there, get busy." And Stevenson got busy, and in a short while a crude steam engine was running down a wooden railroad track. And the world started on wheels, and it's been going on wheels ever since. Ah! my friend, we are living in the time of the end, when knowledge has been increased and men are running to and fro.

It was Sir Isaac Newton, the great scientist and Bible student, who from a study of the prophecies of the Bible predicted that the time would come when man would be able to travel at the speed of 50 miles an hour. Voltaire, the famous infidel, used Newton's prediction as a sure proof of the fallacy of the Bible. "For," said Voltaire, "it shows that a study of the Bible will lead even one of the greatest scientists to make a fool of himself; and to believe the time will come when man will travel at the tremendous speed of 50 miles an hour." Well, Voltaire is dead; Newton is dead; but the Bible lives on, and men are traveling not only 50 miles an hour

Along the Sawdust Trail

but 600 miles an hour. What would Voltaire and Newton think if they could come to life and see men traveling today? Not only at a terrific speed on land but also speeding on aeroplane wings through the air.

Why, do you know that when the locomotive train first came along there were men who tried to get laws passed to prohibit them entirely? It was claimed that they so terrified the horses, cows, and chickens that it would mean the ruination of everything. And when the automobiles first made their appearance on the streets and roads, the men who owned horses hated the automobiles and their owners. For how the horses were terrified when the automobiles came along! Many a man's team was ruined in the awful runaways that occurred. But the prophecies of the Bible foretold that in the *time of the end* the chariots would have flaming torches or lights on them; that they would run like the lightning. So the automobile had to come. Every time you see an automobile, it tells that the Bible is true. Every time the train whistles, it tells us that the Bible is the Word of God and that the prophecies are true and sure. Every time an aeroplane flies over your head, it tells you that we are living in the *time of the end*.

In noticing how the world has been speeded up in the last few years, let us notice the progress and improvement made in the automobile. The first official auto race was held November 28, 1895. There were 60 cars entered in that race, and the distance of the race was 53 1/3 miles. Now what do you suppose was the speed of the winning car? Just guess. Well, out of the 60 cars that entered the race only two succeeded in getting to the end of the 53 1/3 miles. All of the rest had trouble with burned out bearings or the like. And the car that won the race made the terrific speed of 5 1/4 miles per hour. What a race! It reminds one of the old fable about the race between the tortoise and the hare.

But since that time there has been a constant increase in speed. Not so long ago Captain George Edward Thomas Eyston drove his great racing car called the *Thunderbolt* over the racetrack on the salt flats of Utah at the lightning speed of 357 miles per hour.

Why Did God Withhold . . .

"They shall run like lightning," said the prophet 2,500 years ago. Are men running to and fro today? Not so many years ago it took Marcus Whitman *six* months to travel the distance from the state of Washington to the city of Boston. But now men fly from coast to coast in a few hours' time. What a change in just a few short years!

Now, why did God withhold the discovery of all our modern scientific knowledge until the time of the end? And why did He permit all these discoveries, and why did He cause all these wonderful things to be brought to light in these last days in which you and I live? Is it just for man's pleasure and convenience that God has given us all these labor-saving machines, our speedy ways of travel, and our lightning means of communication in the telephone, the telegraph, and the radio? Is it just for man's gratification that the printing press was invented? Oh, no, my friends, let's notice our text in the book of Nahum again. "The chariots shall be with flaming torches in the *day of his preparation*" (Nahum 2:3).

What is meant by the day of God's preparation? The book of Daniel was to be unsealed when the time of the end should begin. And in the time designated as the time of the end, knowledge was to be increased and men run to and fro. So the time of the end is the day of God's preparation. In Matthew 24:14 we read, "And this gospel of the kingdom shall be preached in all the world for a witness unto all nations and then shall the end come." The day of God's preparation is the day when He is sending His gospel as a witness to every nation of the world. In Revelation 14:6, John the revelator tells of what he saw in the prophetic vision. He says, "I saw another angel flying in the midst of heaven having the everlasting gospel to preach unto them that dwell on the earth, to every nation, kindred, tongue and people." God's work of preparation is the sending of the gospel of salvation, the gospel of the kingdom, to all the world. It is His purpose that all men shall have the opportunity to learn about Him, who is the great Creator and Redeemer. The great God of heaven planned a program of

Along the Sawdust Trail

speeding up this old world so that the gospel could be carried to the world in a very short time.

God's enemy, the devil, in his warfare against God, plunged this world into superstition and heathen darkness and attempted to blot the knowledge of God and His truth from the earth. To reveal the results of sin and the awful consequence of rebellion against the government of heaven, God has permitted sin for a time, but iniquity must have an end, and so the Lord says, "We will speed the world up and send the gospel of the kingdom around the world in a short time." In one generation, if you please. And so, when we reached the time of the end, God looked down upon this world and said, "Speed up," and the world began speeding up. How could the everlasting gospel go to all the world, as it says in the twenty-fourth chapter of Matthew, in one generation, by men traveling in oxcarts and sailboats? Why, in the days of the sailboat it took most of a year for word to be taken from one side of the world to the other? Every little community was a world of its own, and very little was known of what went on in the rest of the world. The gospel could never be carried in a short time to all the world with the slow methods of days gone by. When John the revelator was given a view of the everlasting gospel speeding to every nation, he didn't see an oxcart going slowly down a dusty road with the everlasting gospel. And he didn't see an old sailboat sitting in the harbor waiting for the wind to blow. No, he saw an angel flying in the midst of heaven, representing the speed with which the gospel has been carried to all the world since the modern inventions began. Less than a hundred years ago the great heathen nations with their teeming millions had never so much as heard the name of Jesus Christ.

Before the coming of modern inventions, and the invention of the printing press, the Bible had to be copied by hand and could only be had by a favored few. But since the invention of the printing press, the Bible has been printed by the millions of copies and in over 1,000 languages, and the cost of a copy is made so low that everyone who desires to have it may. And with our rapid ways of travel, the missionaries for the last three-fourths of a century have taken the Bible and its wonderful story of God's love and His redeeming grace made possible through the life and death and resurrection of Jesus Christ, to every nation on the globe.

And now you can travel around this world and visit countries where 75 years ago the people were cannibals, and today these same people have been transformed by the gospel from raw, heathen, savage cannibals to loving, tenderhearted Christians. The gospel has been carried to every nation on the earth, during the lifetime of men and women living today. And so the world was speeded up; and the chariots with flaming torches began running like the lightning when we reached the time of the end, the day of God's preparation, when the gospel was to be carried to every nation, kindred, tongue and people.

One more thought—the reason that God didn't permit the discovery of all this scientific knowledge before is this: He knew that sinful men would devote their knowledge of science to the work of destroying human life. While our inventions have been a great blessing, they also turn out to be a terrible curse. Around the world, the nations are all busy working night and day preparing more and more skillful weapons of destruction: and heading on for the last great battle of Armageddon. Since the coming of all those scientific discoveries there have been millions of people who have come to believe that through science and modern inventions the world would soon be made into a veritable paradise and that soon poverty, sickness, pain, disease, famine, and want would be banished from the earth. But, alas! Instead of modern scientific discoveries, bringing this world into a marvelous Utopia, they have brought the most terrible destruction in modern inhuman warfare that has ever been witnessed since the beginning of time. Today there is famine and starvation and death and destruction on a scale that is beyond imagination. The world is being reduced to ruin and disaster. Men are destroying the earth with modern scientific inventions.

In Revelation 11:18, we read, "The nations were angry, and

Along the Sawdust Trail

thy wrath is come, and the time of the dead that they should be judged, and that thou shouldest give reward unto thy servants the prophets, and to the saints, and them that fear thy name, small and great; and shouldest destroy them which destroy the earth." And so the *time of the end* is the *day of God's preparation*; and the end of the reign of sin is near at hand. The admonition of the prophet is: "Prepare to meet thy God."